Zakk Wylde
ANTHOLOGY

Photography by Zakk Wylde except front cover and page 13 by Phil Ciulo

Transcribed by Steve Gorenberg, Jeff Jacobson, and Paul Pappas

Cherry Lane Music Company
Director of Publications/Project Editor: Mark Phillips

ISBN 978-1-60378-393-4

Visit our website at www.cherrylaneprint.com

BETWEEN HEAVEN AND HELL

Written by Zachary Wylde

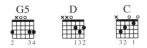

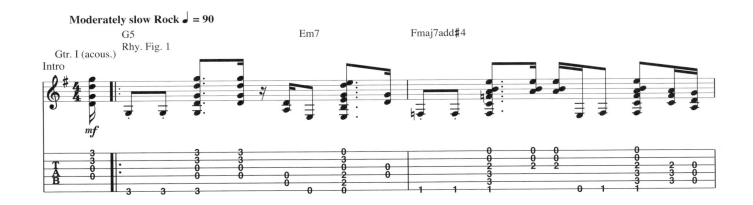

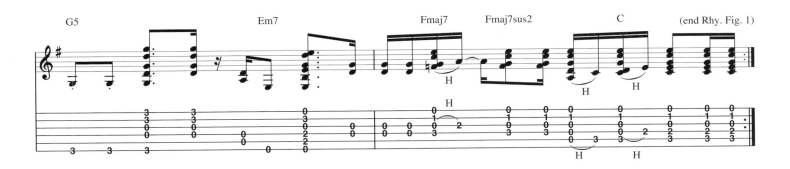

1. Dy-ing to live,_ liv-ing to_____ die._ Ain't no hel-los_ here,
2. *See additional lyrics*

noth-ing but good-byes.___ It's like sing-ing a song_ that can-not be_____ sung.___

It's like hav-ing to end,____ child,___ what's yet to have____ be-gun.___ Lord._____

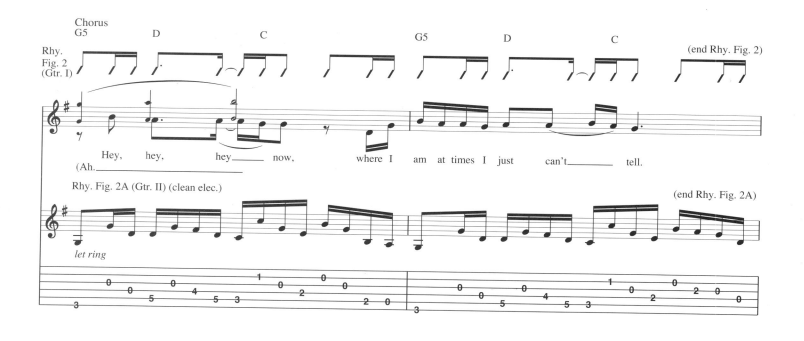

Hey, hey, hey_____ now, where I am at times I just can't_____ tell.
(Ah._____

Hey, hey, hey__ now, I'm lost_____ some-where be-tween heav-en and hell.__
Ah.)_____

Mm._____

(Spoken:) Somewhere.

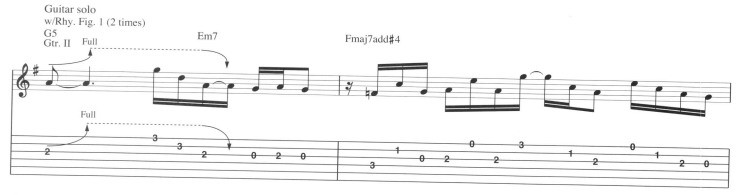

Outro

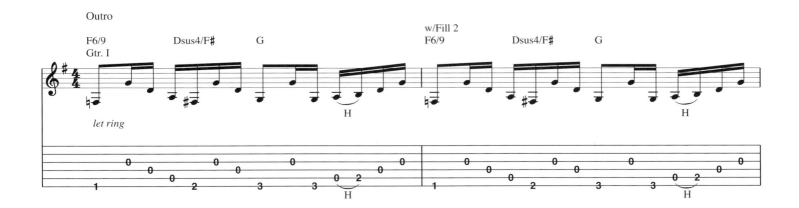

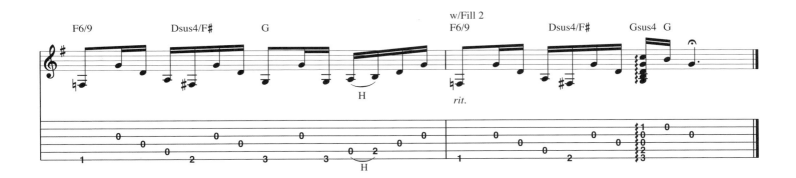

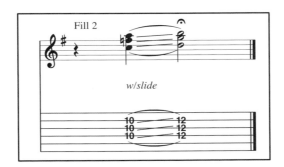

Additional Lyrics

2. All that you know and all that you knew,
   In the end, child, tell me, what's it all mean to you?
   Don't forget just who and where you are.
   You can spread your wings, son, but don't you spread yourself too far. *(To Chorus)*

BLEED FOR ME

Written by Zachary Wylde

Drop D tuning, down 1 step:
(low to high) C-G-C-F-A-D

Intro
Moderate Rock ♩ = 122

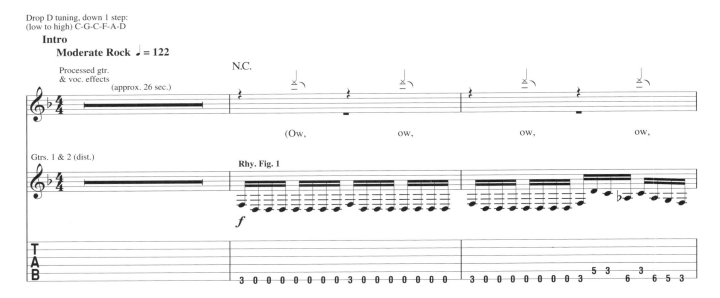

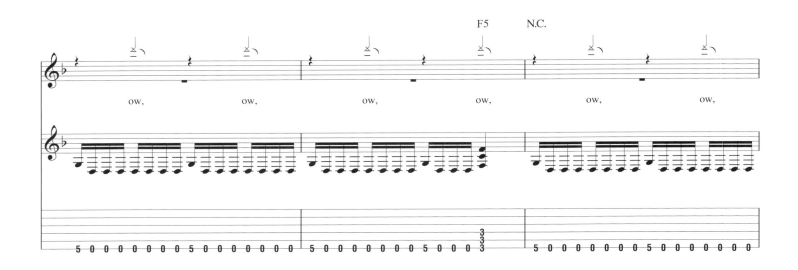

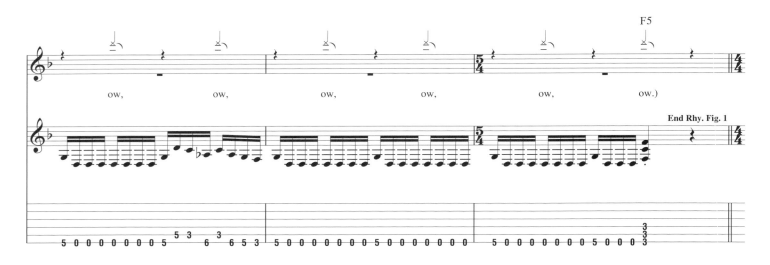

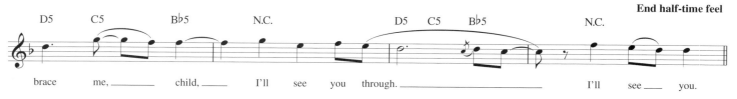

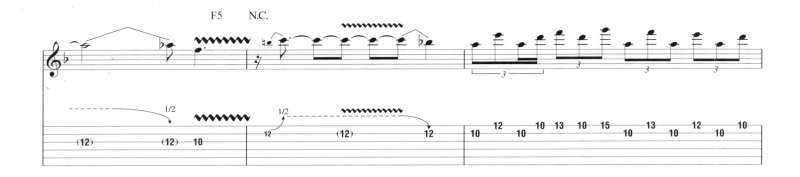

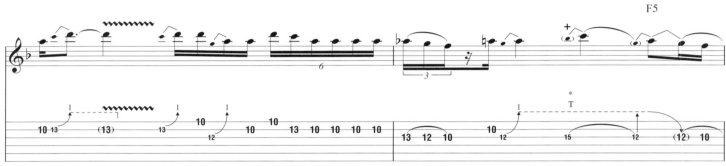

*Hold bend while tapping and pulling off with right hand.

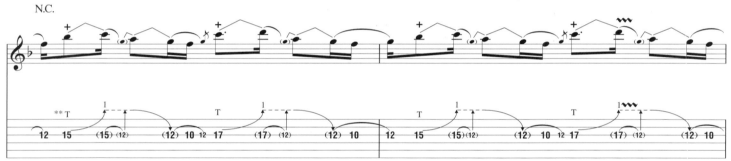

**Tap note then bend w/ left hand.

D.S.S. al Coda 2

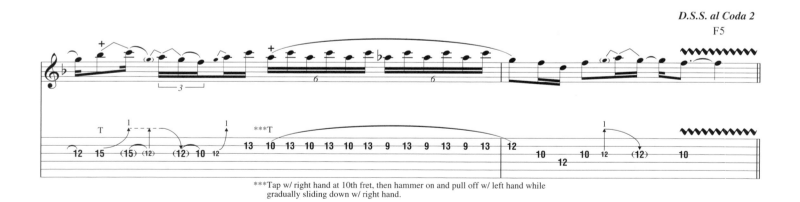

***Tap w/ right hand at 10th fret, then hammer on and pull off w/ left hand while gradually sliding down w/ right hand.

Coda 2

F5

ow,   ow,   ow,   ow.)

THE BLESSED HELLRIDE

Written by Zachary Wylde

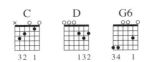

Drop D tuning:
(low to high) D-A-D-G-B-E

Intro

Moderately slow Rock ♩ = 76

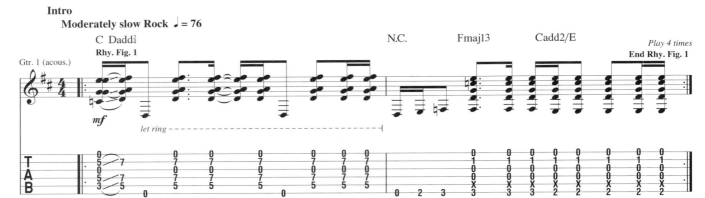

Verse

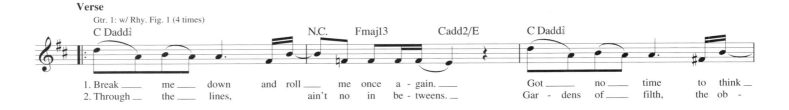

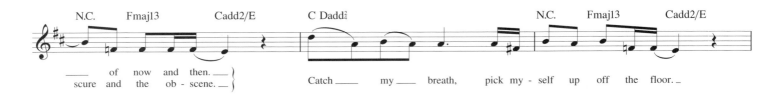

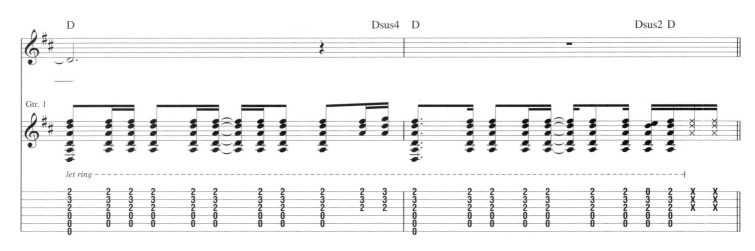

1. Break ___ me ___ down and roll ___ me once a - gain. ___ Got ___ no ___ time to think
2. Through ___ the ___ lines, ___ ain't no in be - tweens. ___ Gar - dens of ___ filth, the ob -

___ of now and then. ___
scure and the ob - scene. ___

Catch ___ my ___ breath, pick my - self up off the floor. ___

One ___ more ___ drink, ___ a nerv - ous break - down, then ___ an - oth - er war. ___

Chorus

Oh, you can nev - er get too _____ low _____ when you're so damn _____

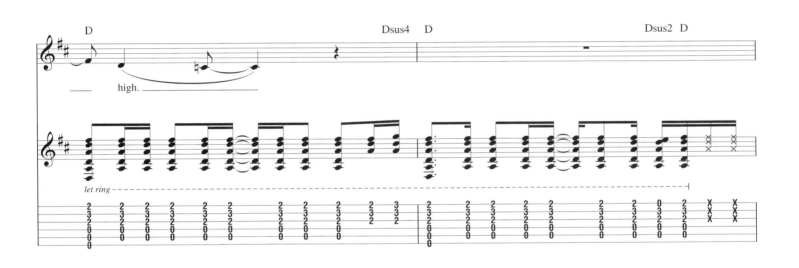

_____ high. _____

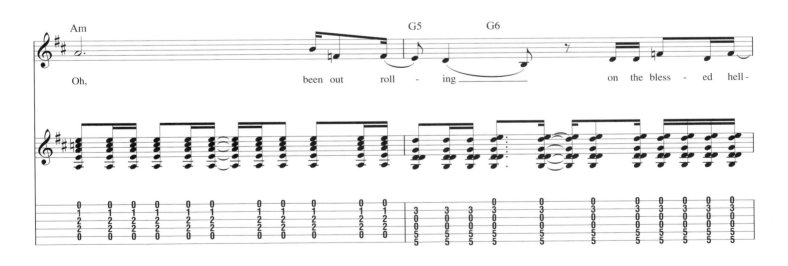

Oh, been out roll - ing _____ on the bless - ed hell-

1.

Gtr. 1: w/ Rhy. Fig. 1 (2 times)

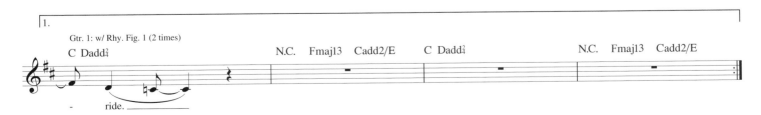

- ride. _____

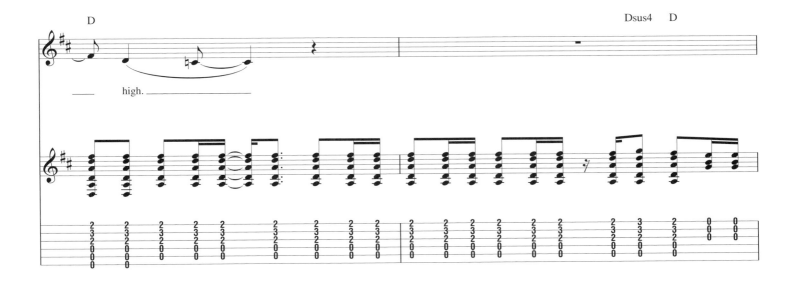

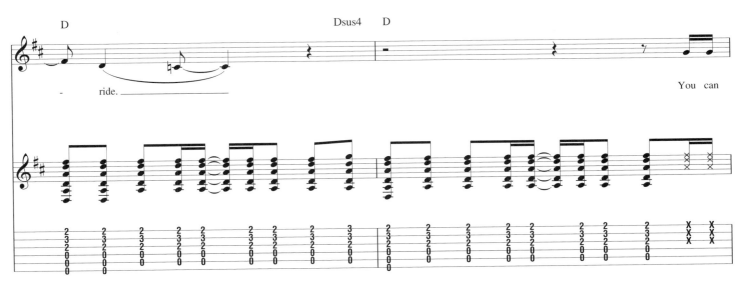

19

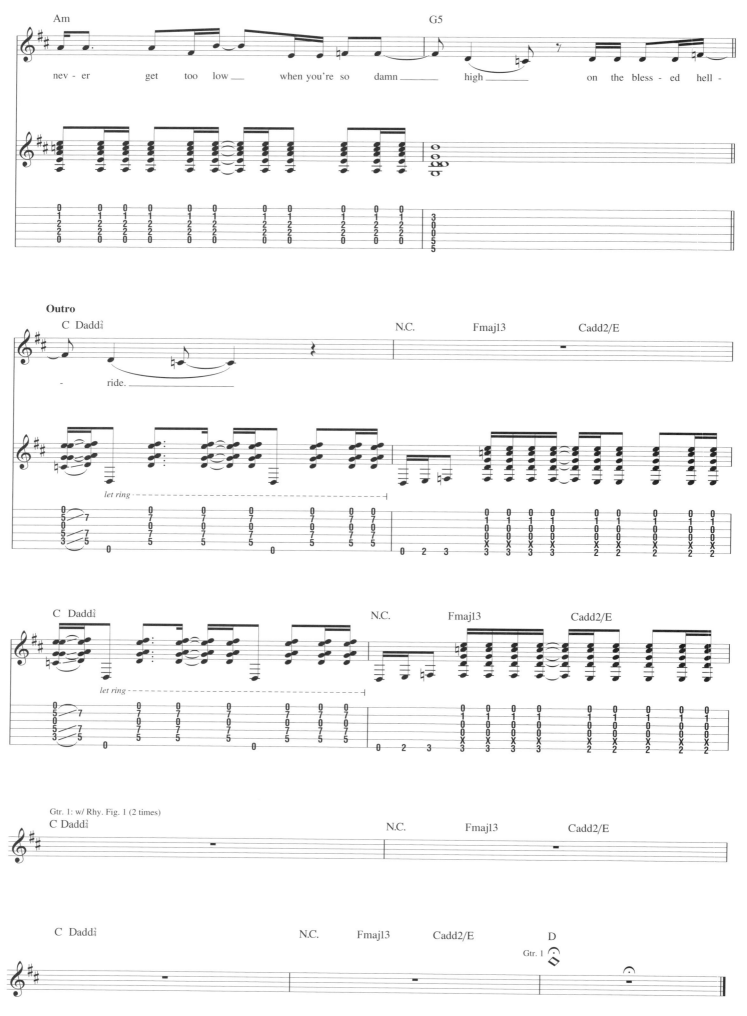

BORED TO TEARS

Written by Zachary Wylde

Shot my drugs,___ drank my booze.___ Tired of joy___ and___ self a - buse.___ E -

ter - nal - ly jad - ed through and through.___ Just a self - loath - ing dick with - out___ a clue.___
(Oh.)_____

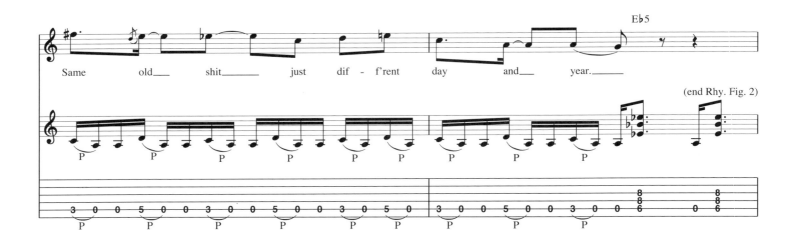

Chorus
N.C.

Bored to___ death.___ Oh, I'm just bored_ to___ tears.___

Rhy. Fig. 2 (Gtr. II)

Same old___ shit_____ just dif - f'rent day and___ year.___

w/Rhy. Fig. 2
N.C.

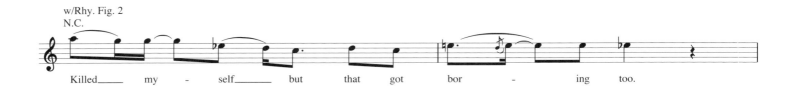

Killed_____ my - self_____ but that got bor - ing too.

To Coda

So be - yond_____ the point where it's not____ true.___

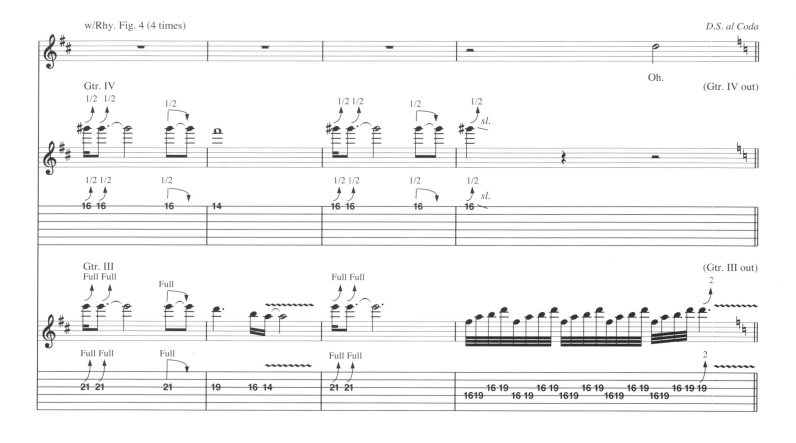

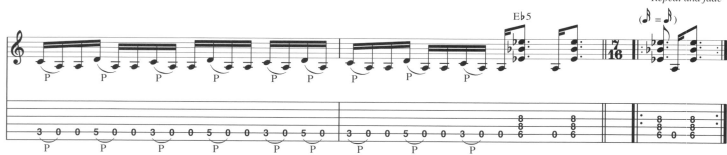

Additional Lyrics

2. Far beyond high, dramatically low.
   Eternal stare, as if I care to know.
   All of this struggle, all of this work.
   In the end you die like some moronic jerk.
   Shot my drugs, drank my booze.
   Tired of joy and self abuse.
   Eternally jaded through and through.
   Just a self-loathing fuck without a clue. *(To Chorus)*

CONCRETE JUNGLE

Written by
Zachary Wylde

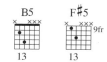

Tune down 1 step:
(low to high) D-G-C-F-A-D

Intro

Moderate Rock ♩ = 138

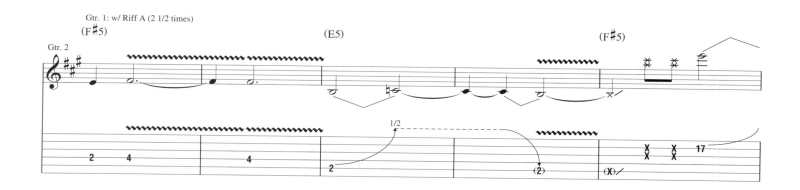

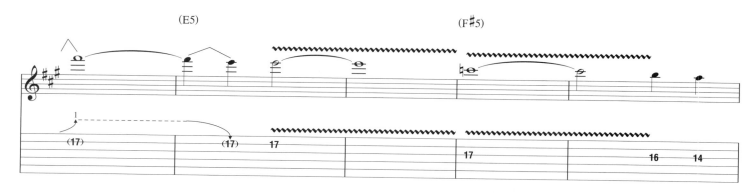

ain't no pit - y. No one gets out a - live. _____
mag - gots play God, where the souls of the lost come _____

_____ to die. In the con - crete jun - gle it's the well of the damned. _ Won't you

step in - side _____ and then you'll un - der - stand. _ Mis - fits, psy - chos, and the

twist - ed slaves, _ the house of the sane, no one can be saved. _

Pre-Chorus

N.C.(B5)   Csus#4   N.C.(B5)

Gtr. 3: w/ Rhy. Fig. 3 (2 times)

Roll - ing six feet un - der, roll - ing.   Roll - ing six feet un - der, roll -

Gtr. 1   **Riff B**

w/ chorus

Gtr. 3   **Rhy. Fig. 3**   **End Rhy. Fig. 3**

P.M. ------------

Csus#4   N.C.(B5)   Csus#4

- ing.   Roll - ing six feet un - der, roll _____ and keep on roll - ing. _____

Gtr. 1   **End Riff B**

28

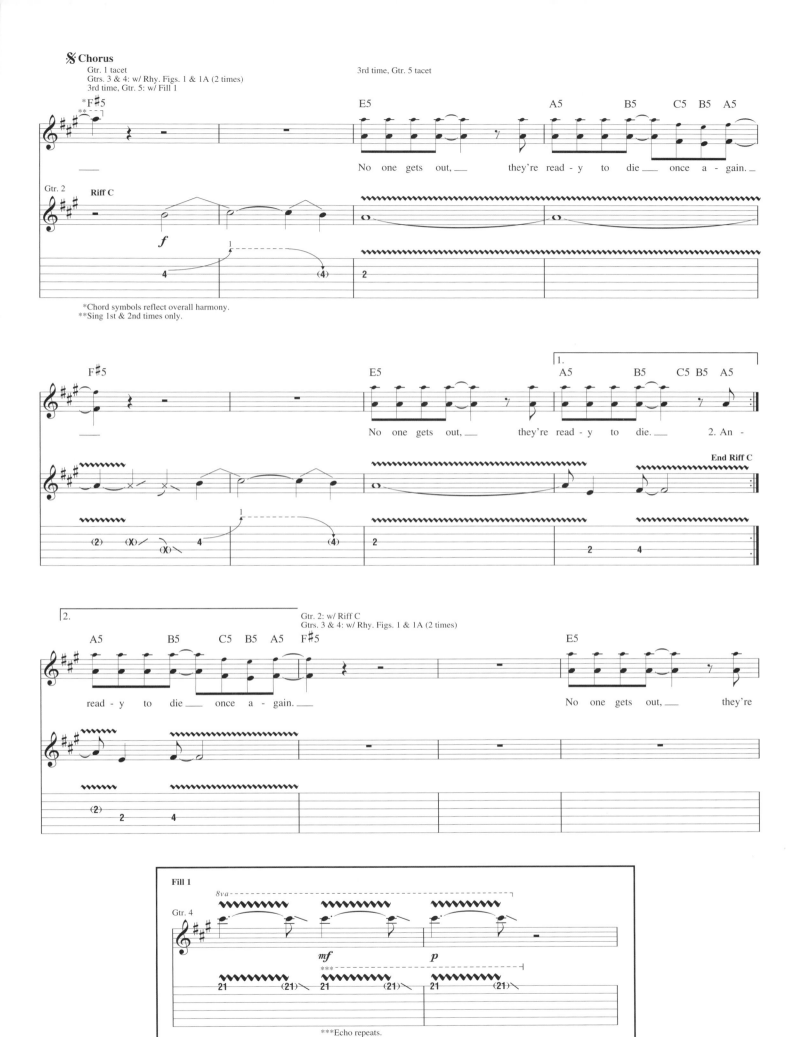

Guitar Solo
Gtr. 1: w/ Riff B
Gtrs. 2 & 4 tacet
Gtr. 3: w/ Rhy. Fig. 3 (3 times)

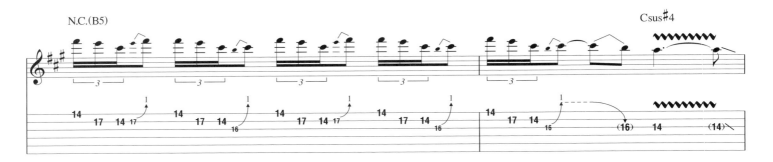

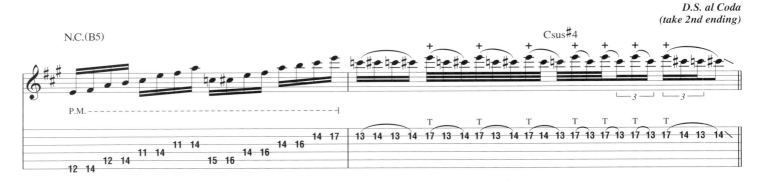

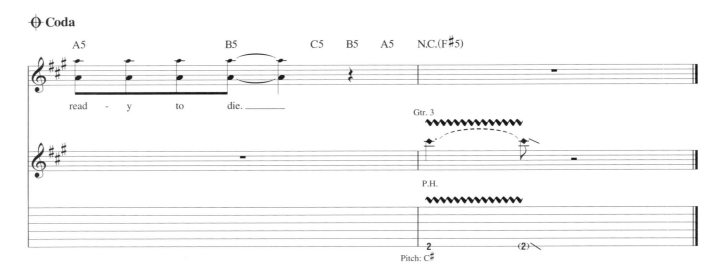

DARKEST DAYS
(Unplugged Version)

Written by
Zachary Wylde

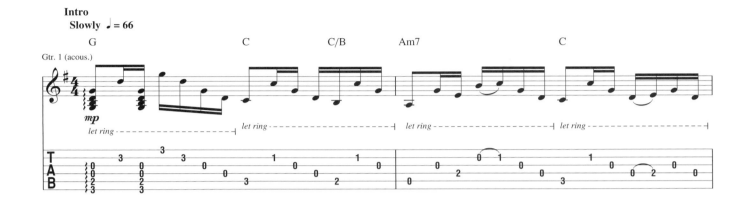

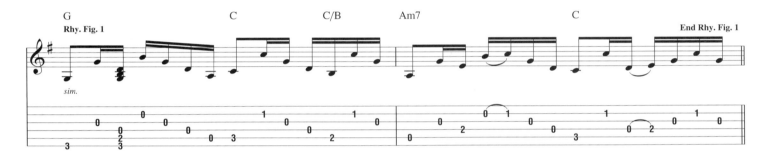

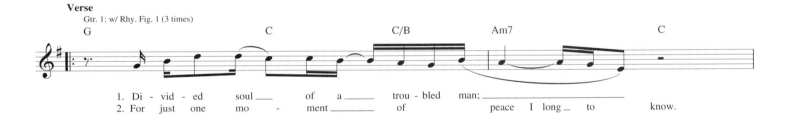

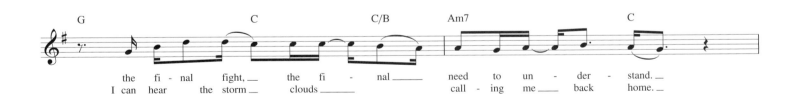

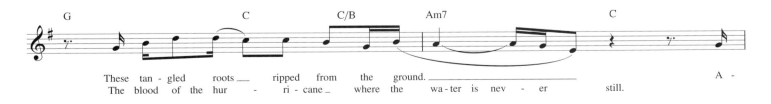

1. Di - vid - ed soul of a trou - bled man;
2. For just one mo - ment of peace I long to know.

the fi - nal fight, the fi - nal need to un - der - stand.
I can hear the storm clouds call - ing me back home.

These tan - gled roots ripped from the ground. A -
The blood of the hur - ri - cane where the wa - ter is nev - er still.

ban - don - ment _ and wor - ry _ for - ev - er to _ be found. _
Life is a load - ed _ gun; _ love is a bul - let that some - times kills.

Gtr. 1

let ring ----------- let ring -------------- let ring ------------ let ring --------

𝄋 Chorus

3rd time, Gtr. 3: w/ Fill 1

Rain. _____ Rain. _____ Rain. _____ Rain. _____

Rhy. Fig. 2

let ring -------------- let ring ----------- let ring ----------

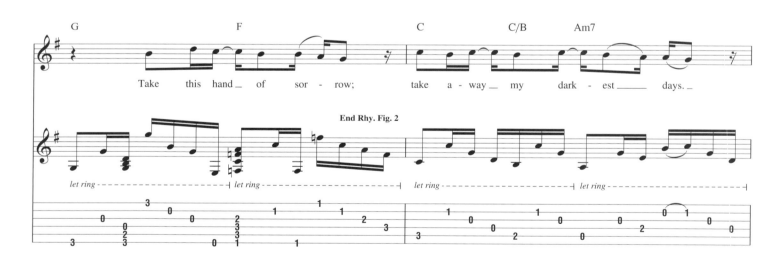

Take this hand _ of sor - row; take a - way _ my dark - est _____ days. _

End Rhy. Fig. 2

let ring --------------- let ring ------- let ring --------------- let ring --------

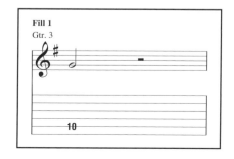

Fill 1
Gtr. 3

10

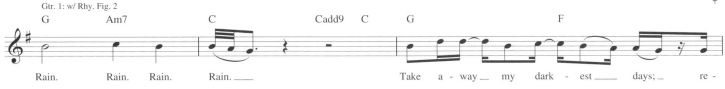

Gtr. 1: w/ Rhy. Fig. 2

Rain. Rain. Rain. Rain. ___ Take a - way ___ my dark - est ___ days; ___ re -

1.

turn me for ___ I feel ___ they're here ___ to stay. ___

Gtr. 1

let ring ___ *let ring* ___ *sim.*

Rhy. Fig. 3

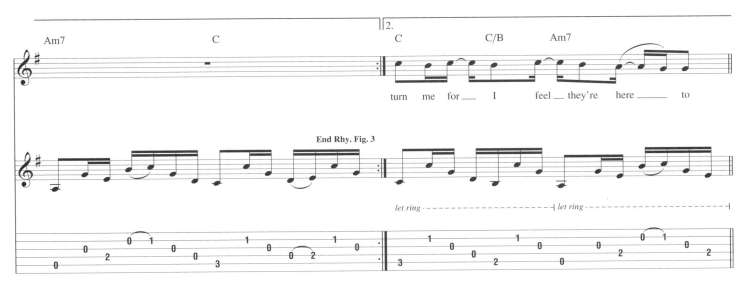

2.

turn me for ___ I feel ___ they're here ___ to

End Rhy. Fig. 3

let ring ___ *let ring* ___

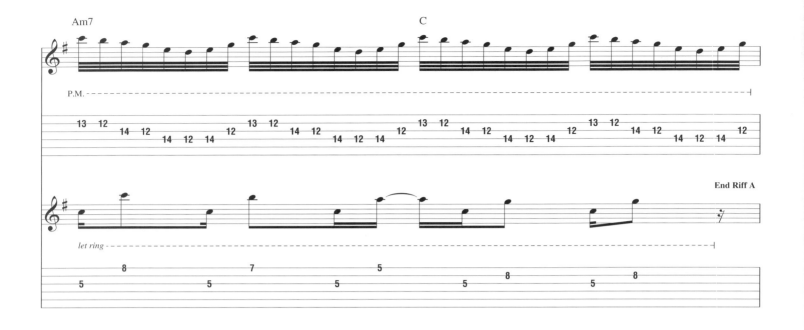

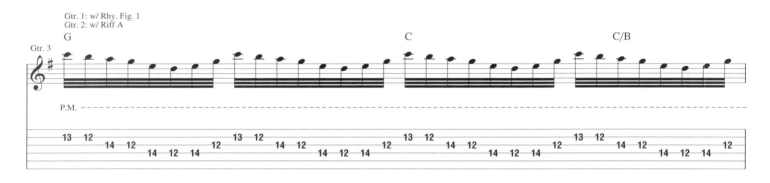

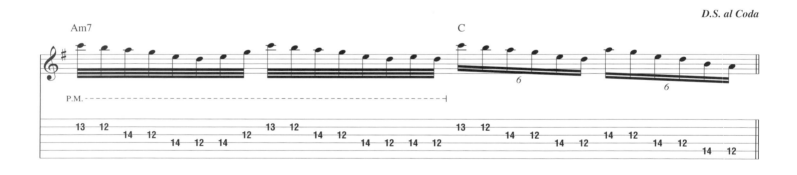

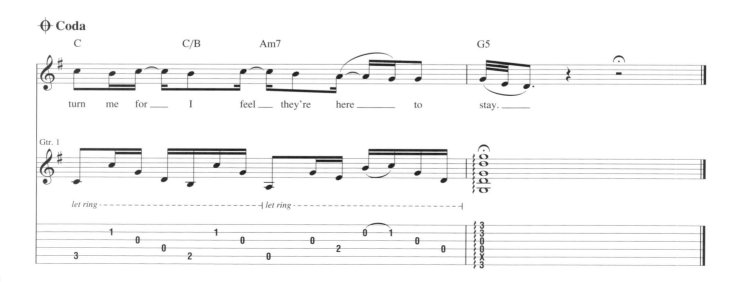

FIRE IT UP

Written by
Zachary Wylde

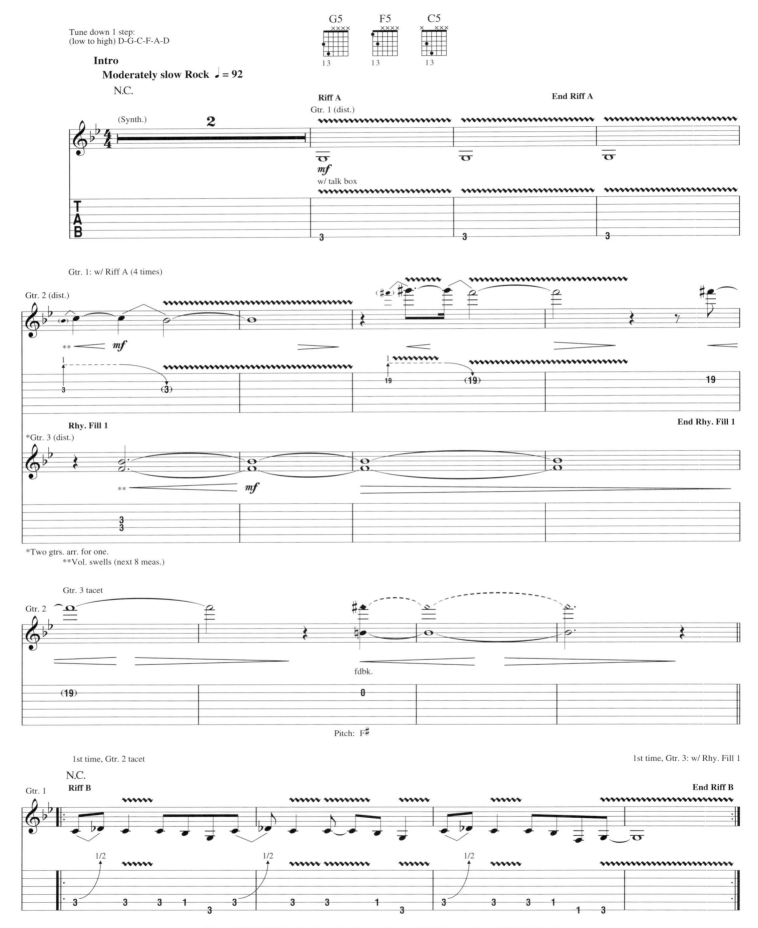

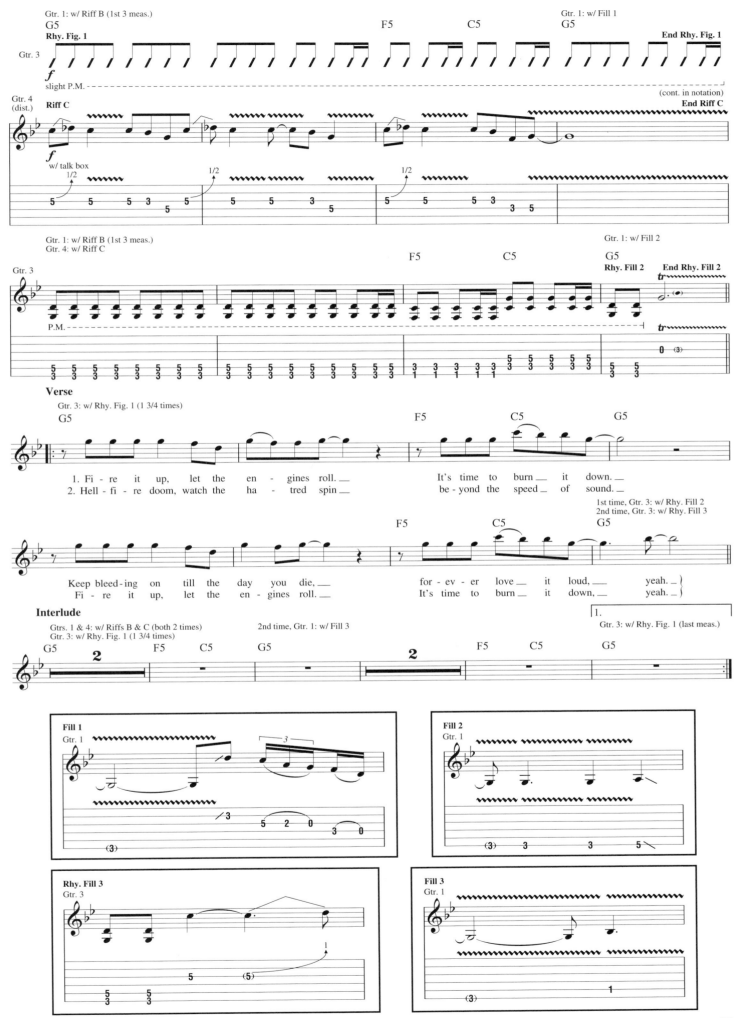

*While trilling, slide palm of right hand across
3rd string producing random harmonics.

Guitar Solo

Gtr. 3: w/ Rhy. Fig. 1 (2 times)

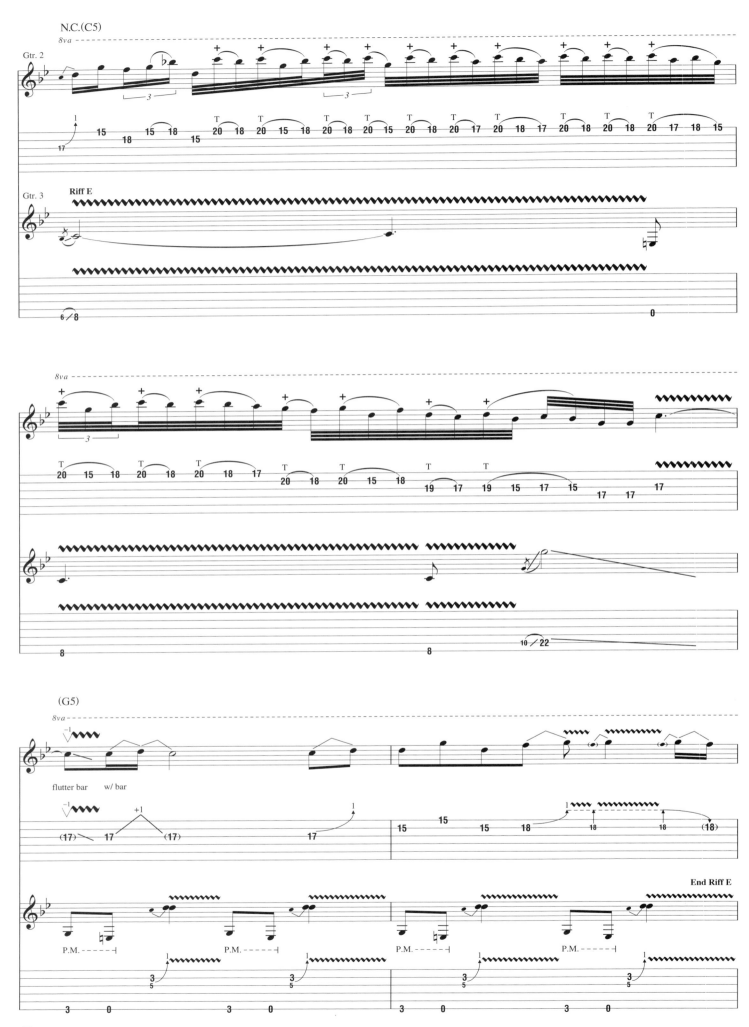

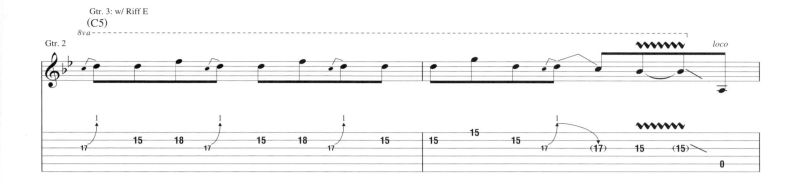

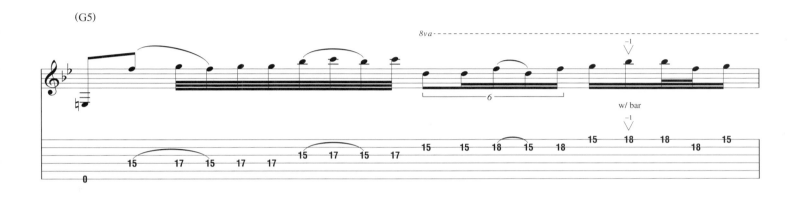

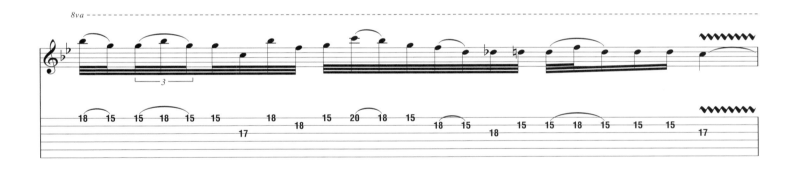

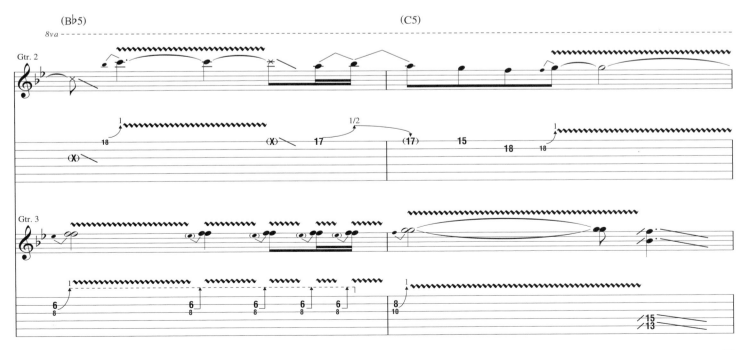

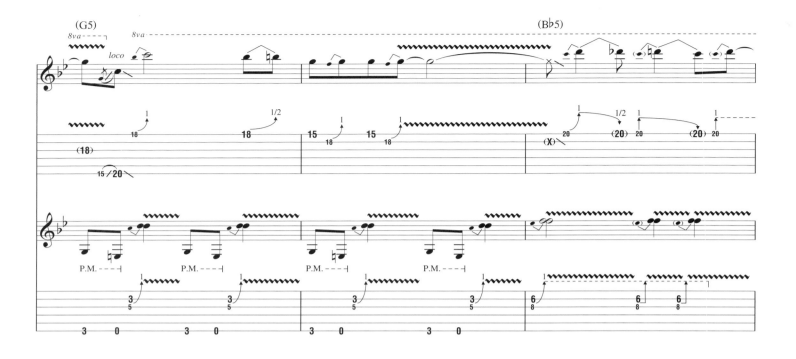

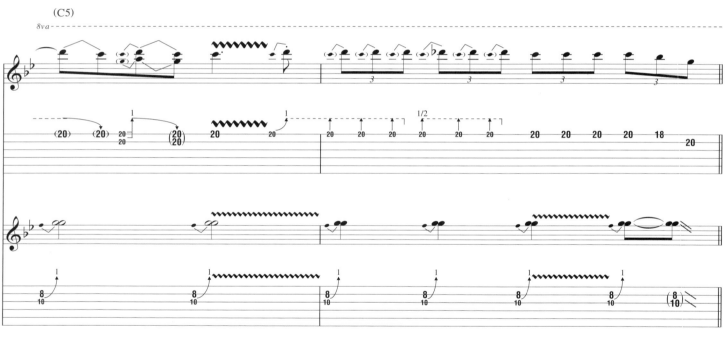

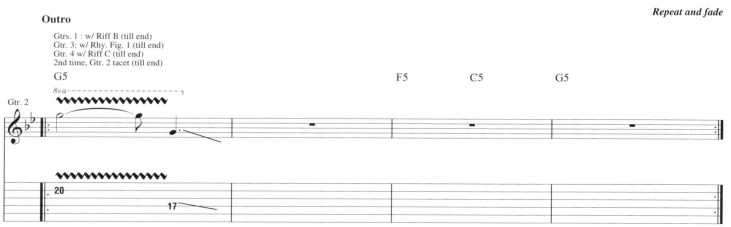

44

THE FIRST NOEL

Written by
Zachary Wylde

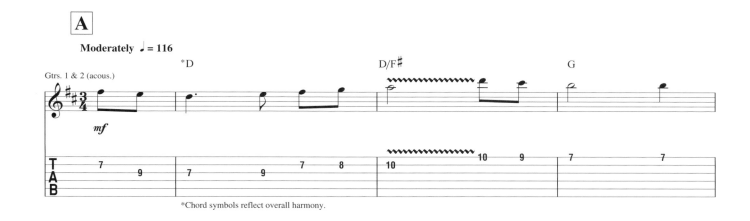

*Chord symbols reflect overall harmony.

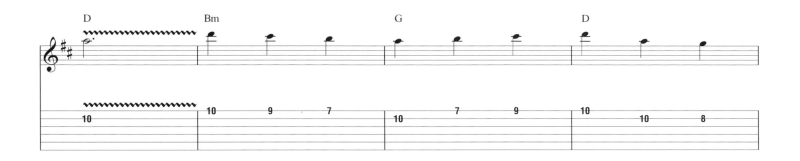

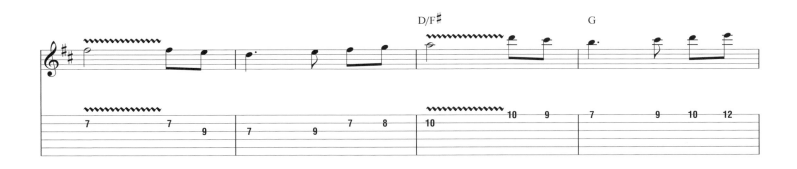

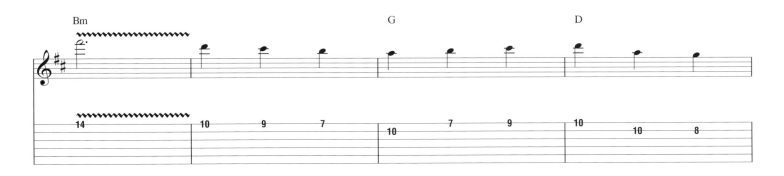

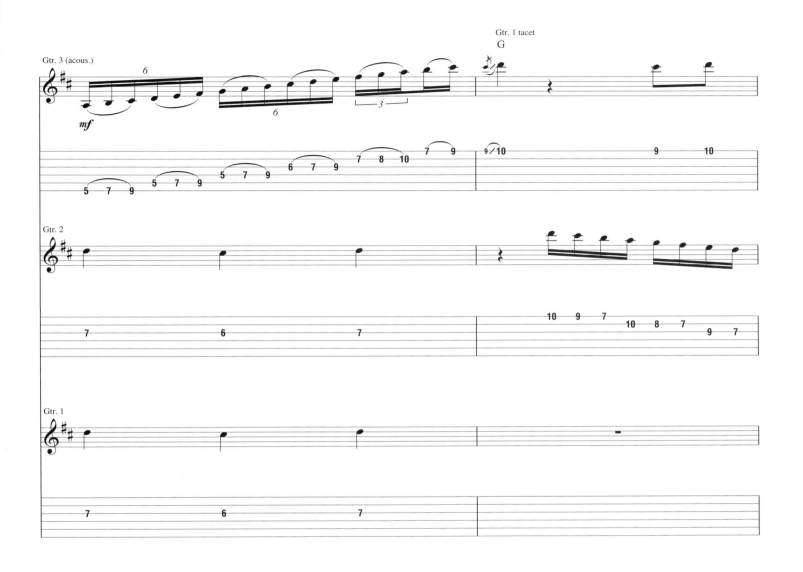

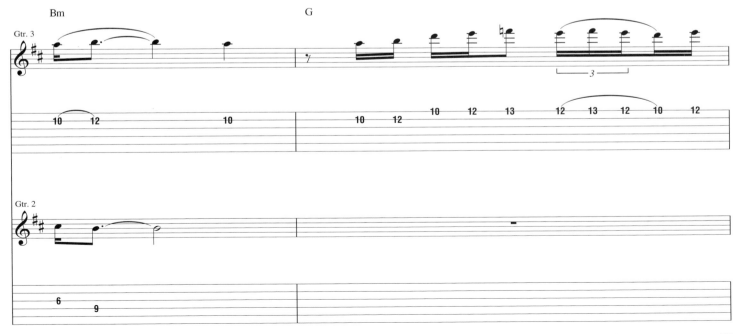

47

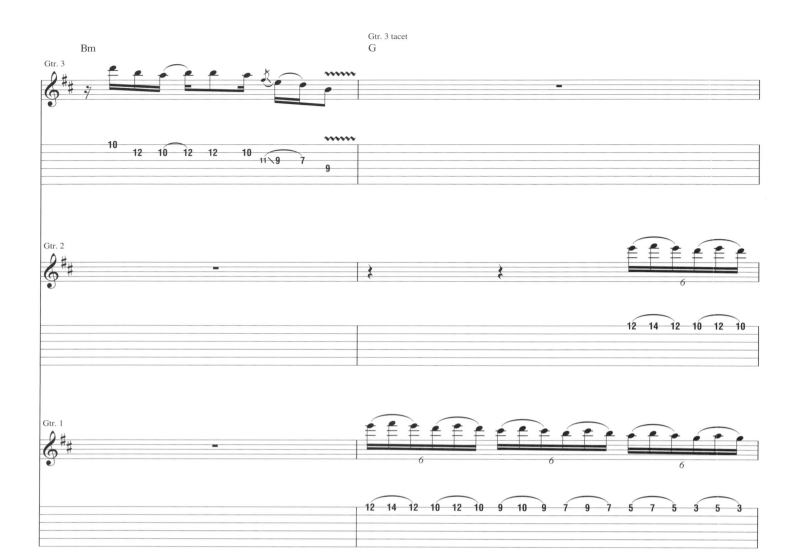
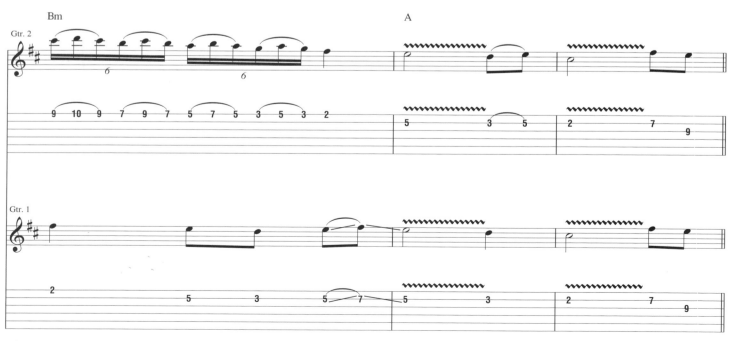

48

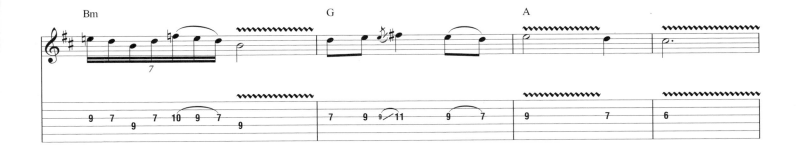

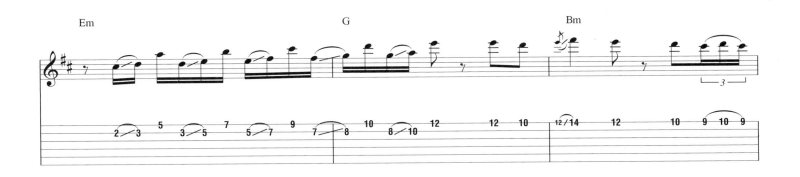

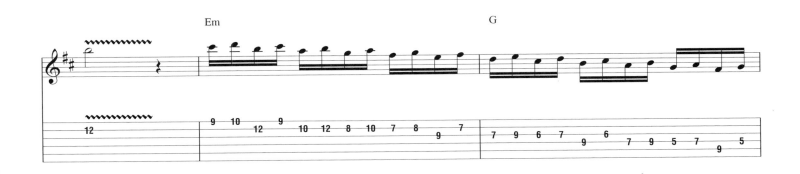

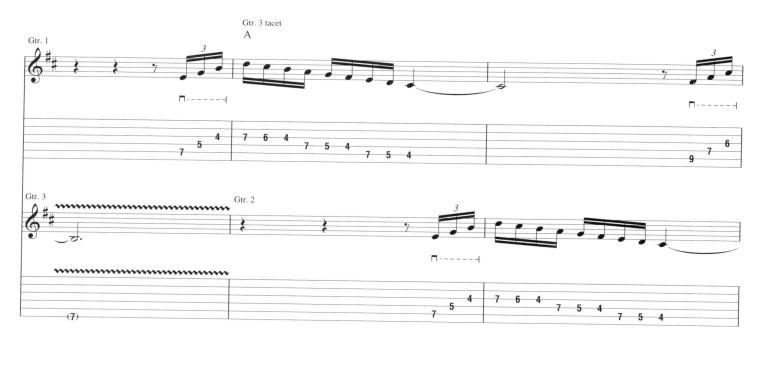

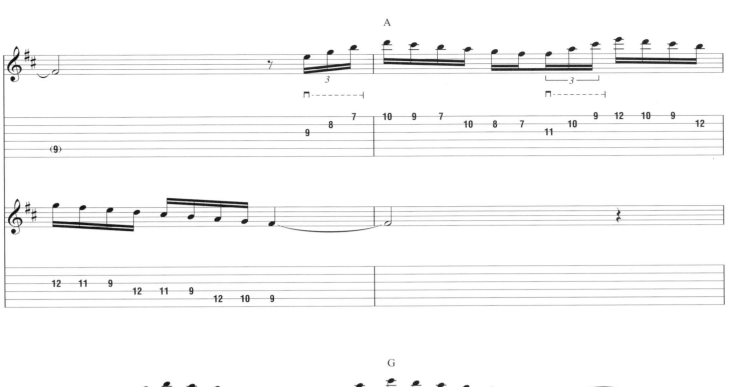

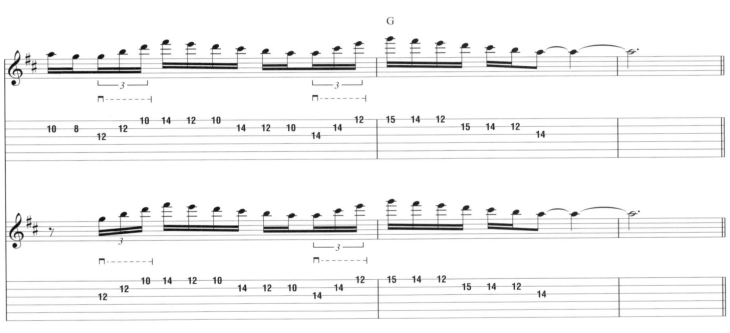

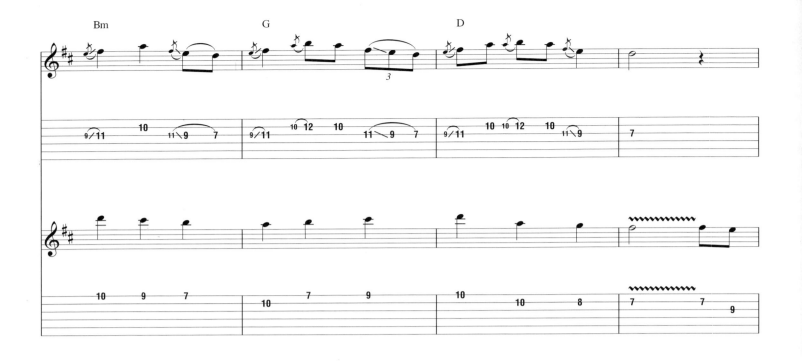

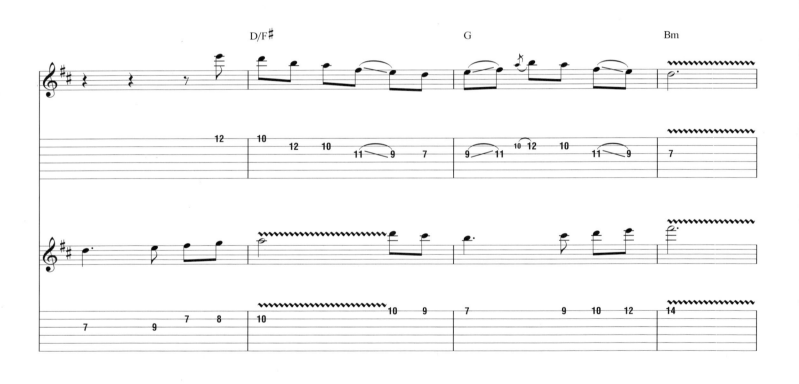

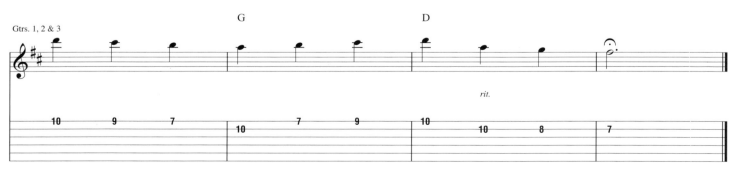

54

FUNERAL BELL

Written by
Zachary Wylde

Drop B tuning, down 1/2 step:
(low to high) Bb-Ab-Db-Gb-Bb-Eb

Intro
Moderately ♩ = 112

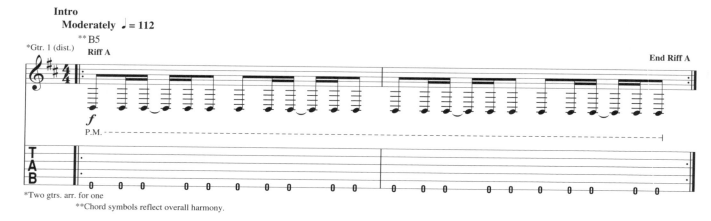

*Two gtrs. arr. for one
**Chord symbols reflect overall harmony.

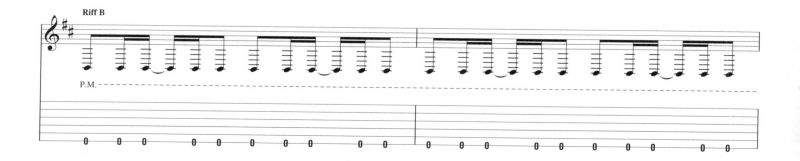

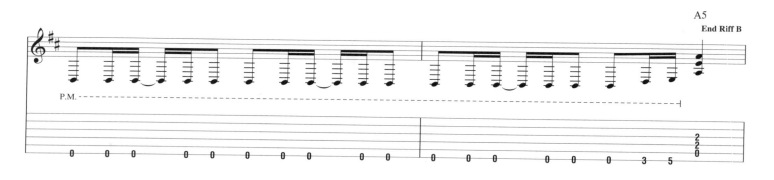

***Doubled throughout

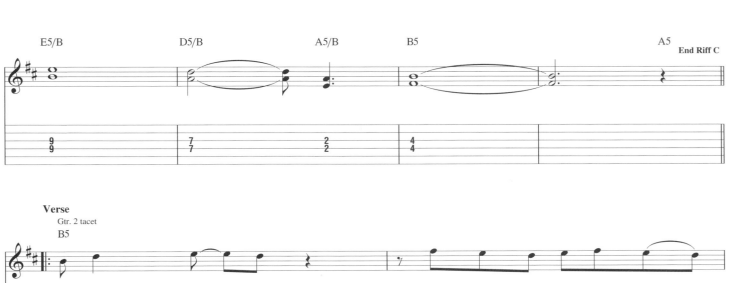

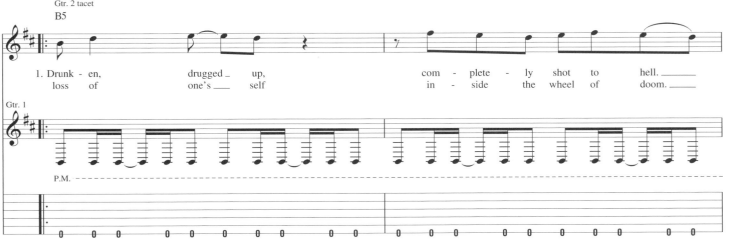

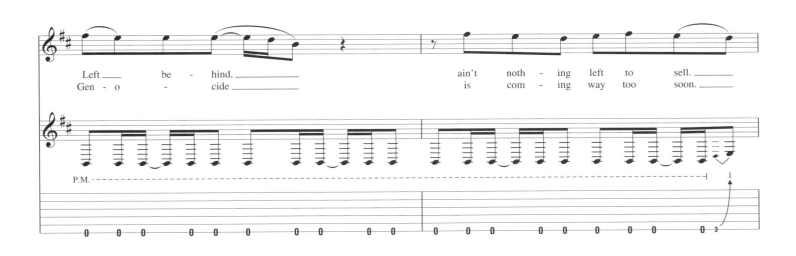

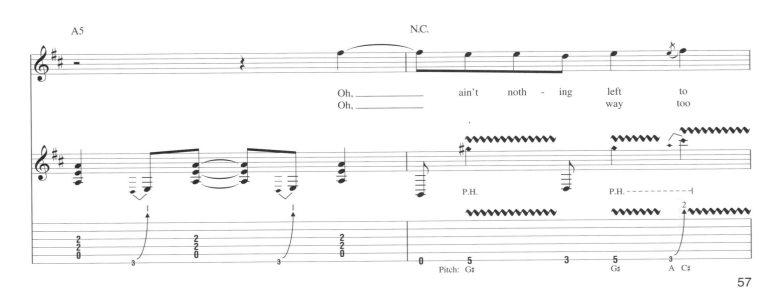

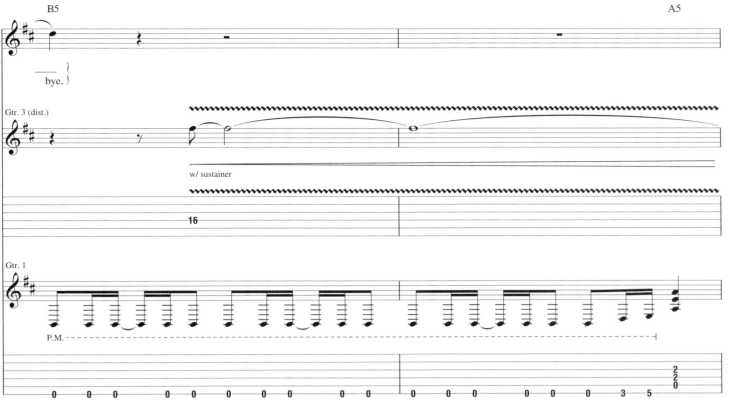

2nd time, Gtr. 1: w/ Fill 1

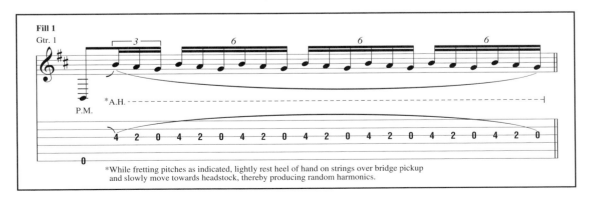

*While fretting pitches as indicated, lightly rest heel of hand on strings over bridge pickup
and slowly move towards headstock, thereby producing random harmonics.

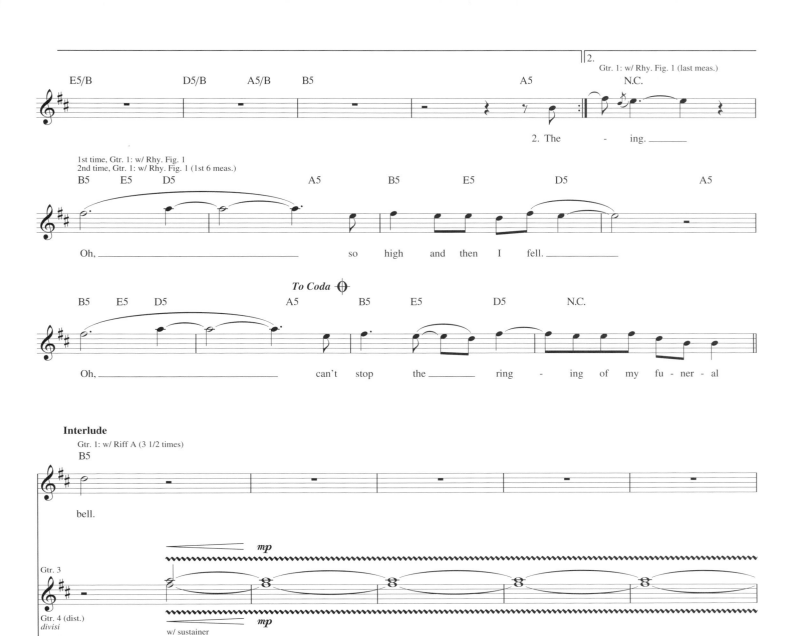

E5/B   D5/B   A5/B   B5   A5   N.C.

2. The   - ing.

1st time, Gtr. 1: w/ Rhy. Fig 1
2nd time, Gtr. 1: w/ Rhy. Fig. 1 (1st 6 meas.)
B5   E5   D5   A5   B5   E5   D5   A5

Oh,   so   high and then I   fell.

To Coda ⊕

B5   E5   D5   A5   B5   E5   D5   N.C.

Oh,   can't stop the   ring - ing of my fu - ner - al

Interlude

Gtr. 1: w/ Riff A (3 1/2 times)
B5

bell.

Gtr. 3

Gtr. 4 (dist.)
divisi
w/ sustainer

10
11

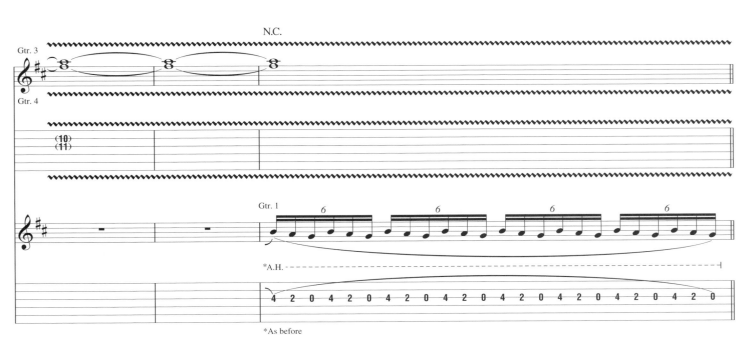

Gtr. 3

Gtr. 4

(10)
(11)

Gtr. 1
6   6   6   6

*A.H.

4 2 0 4 2 0 4 2 0 4 2 0 4 2 0 4 2 0 4 2 0 4 2 0

*As before

Guitar Solo

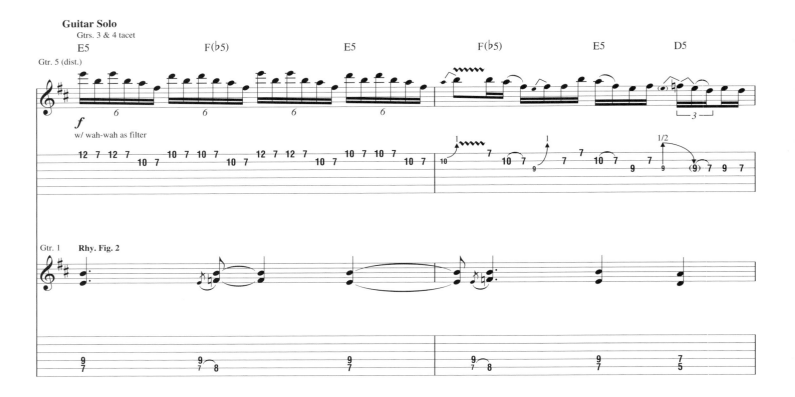

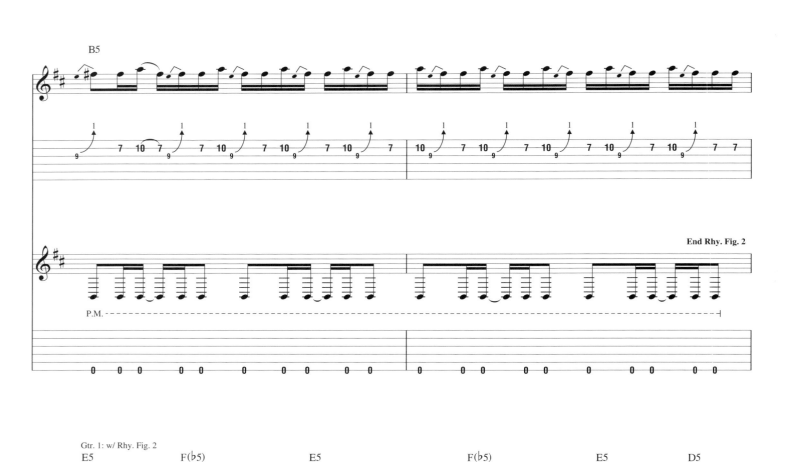

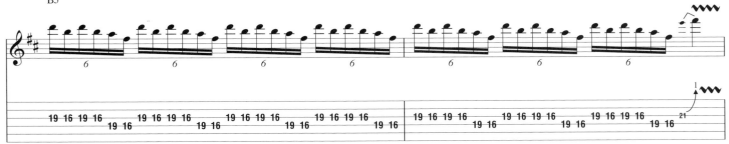

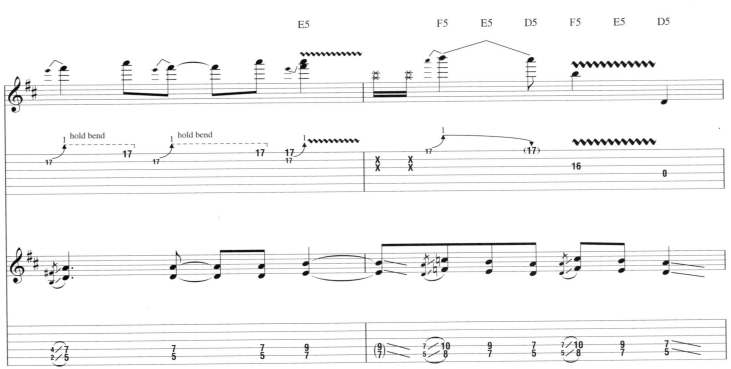

stop the ____ ring — ing of my fu — ner — al

bell.

Pitch: C#
**Refers to harmonic only.

HELL IS HIGH

Written by
Zachary Wylde

G5

Drop D tuning:
(low to high) D-A-D-G-B-E

Intro
Moderate Rock ♩ = 138
N.C.

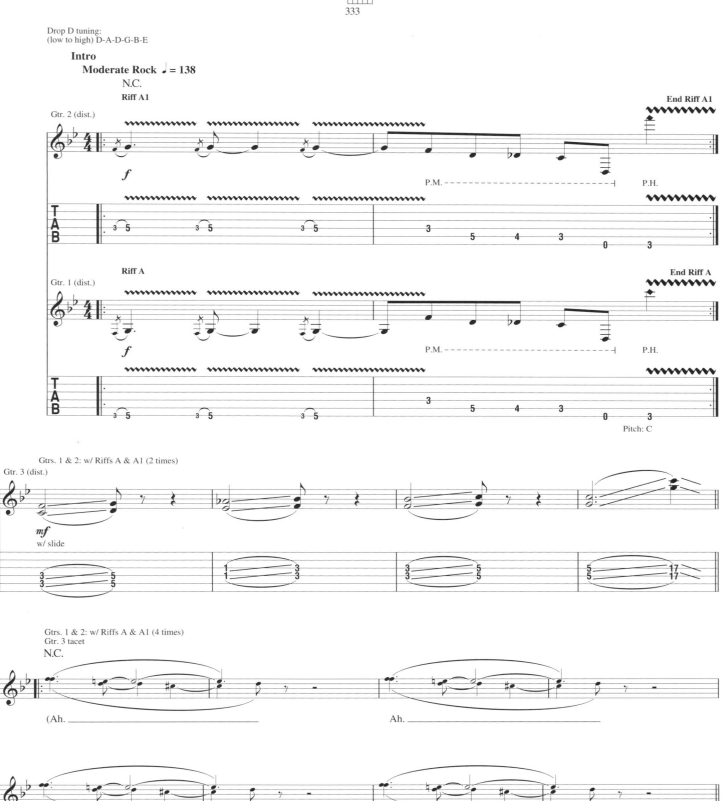

Gtrs. 1 & 2: w/ Riffs A & A1 (8 times)

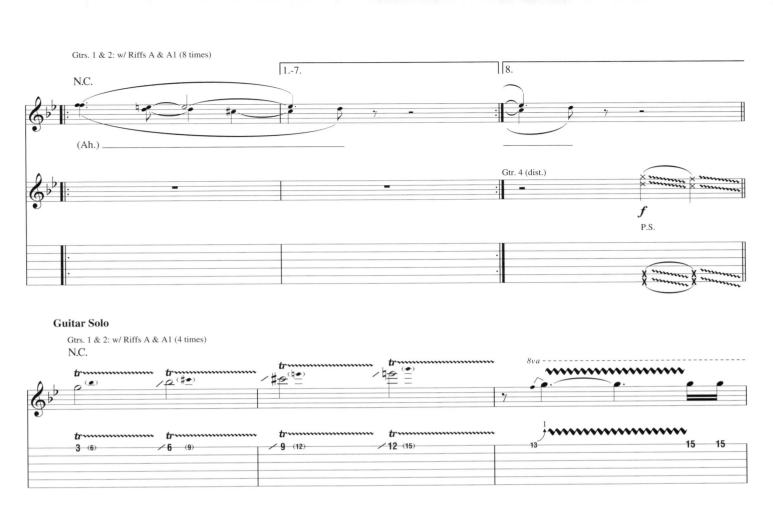

Guitar Solo

Gtrs. 1 & 2: w/ Riffs A & A1 (4 times)

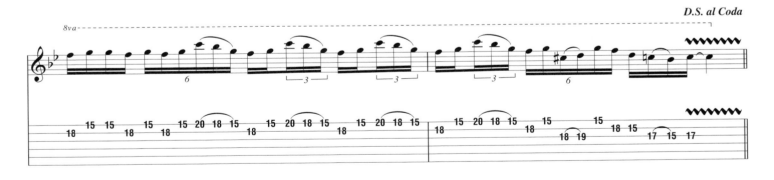

D.S. al Coda

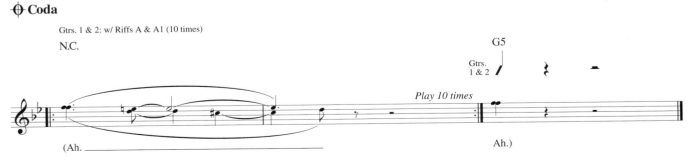

Coda

Gtrs. 1 & 2: w/ Riffs A & A1 (10 times)

67

I DON'T WANT TO CHANGE THE WORLD

Words and Music by
Ozzy Osbourne, Zakk Wylde,
Randy Castillo and Lemmy Kilmister

Tune down 1/2 step:
(low to high) E♭-A♭-D♭-G♭-B♭-E♭

Intro

Moderately fast Rock ♩ = 126

* Chord symbols reflect basic harmony.

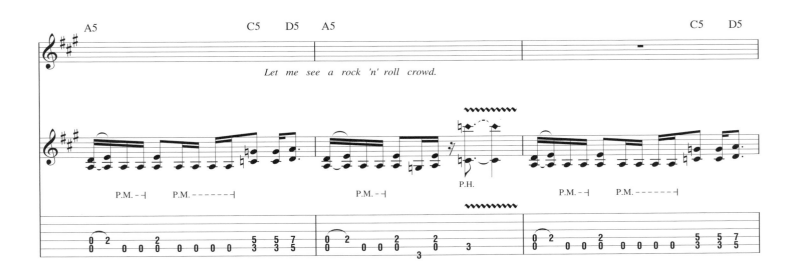

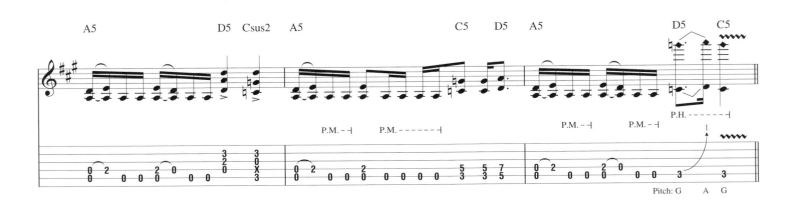

Verse

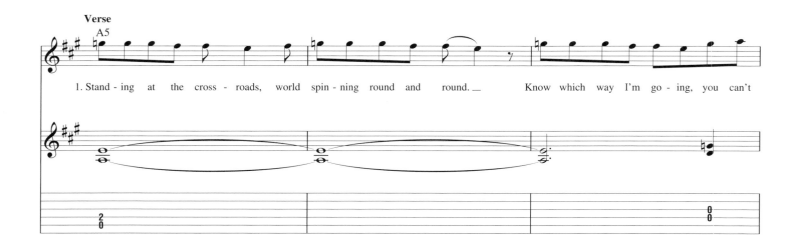

1. Stand - ing at the cross - roads, world spin - ning round and round. __ Know which way I'm go - ing, you can't

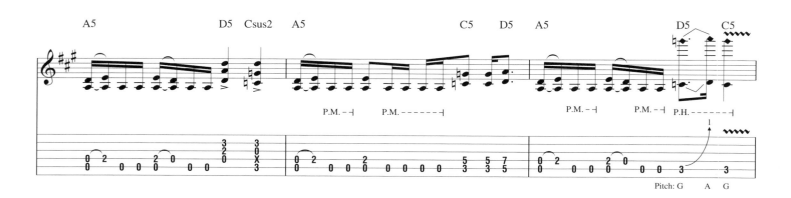

bring _____ me _____ down. _____

* Lightly rest the edge of the R.H. palm perpendicular to and across the strings.
  Starting at the pickups, steadily slide the palm down the fretboard while the L.H. performs the indicated pulloffs.

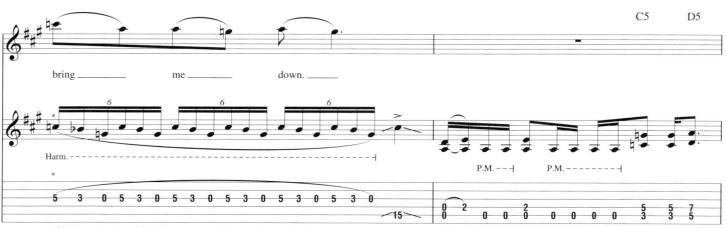

Pitch: G   A   G

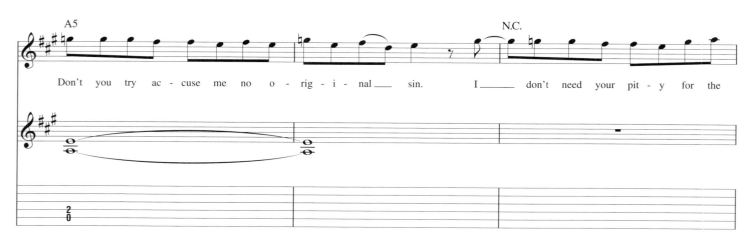

Don't you try ac - cuse me no o - rig - i - nal __ sin. I __ don't need your pit - y for the

Interlude

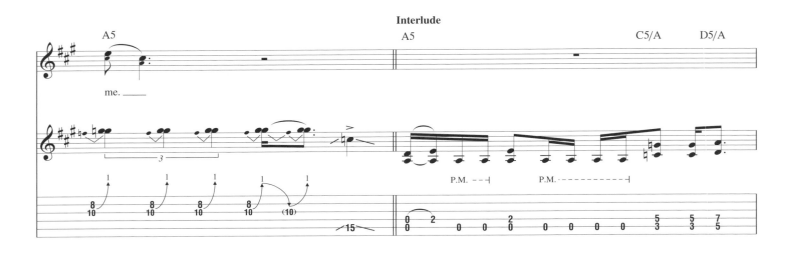

me. _____

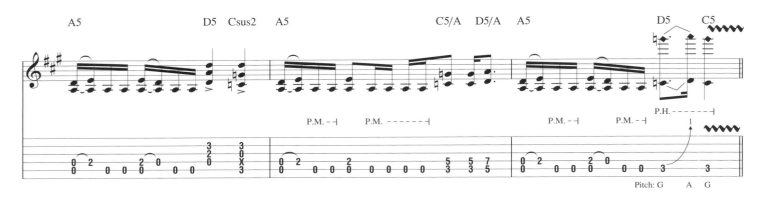

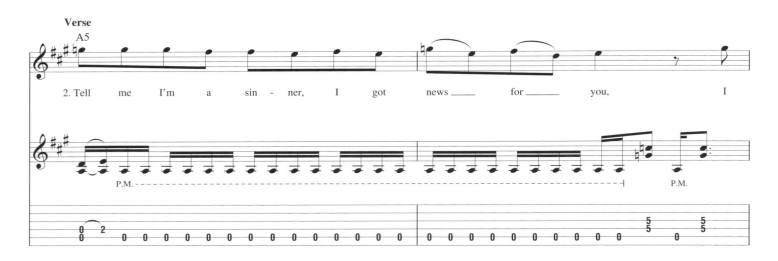

Verse

2. Tell me I'm a sin-ner, I got news _____ for _____ you, I

spoke to God this morn-ing and He don't _____ like _____ you. _____ You're

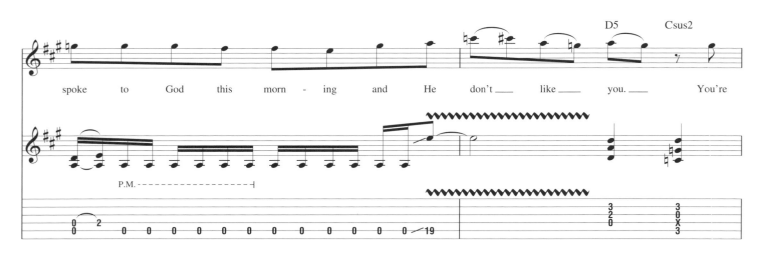

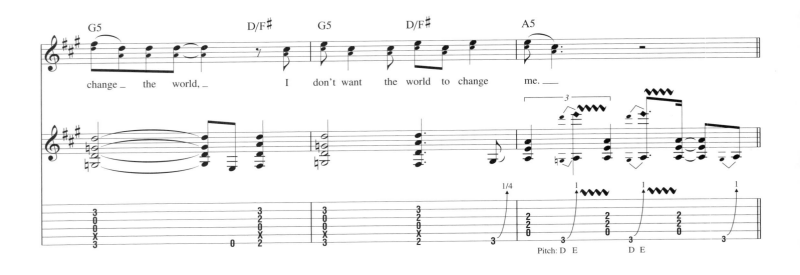

change _ the world, I don't want the world to change me. _

Pitch: D E D E

Bridge

You know it ain't eas - y. _

Rhy. Fig. 2

End Rhy. Fig. 2

P.M.

Gtr. 1: w/ Rhy. Fig. 2 (3 times)

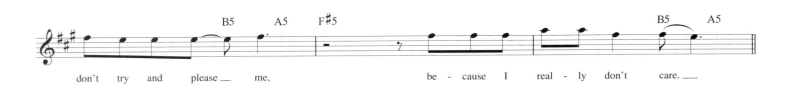

You know it ain't fair. _ So

don't try and please _ me, be - cause I real - ly don't care. _

Guitar Solo

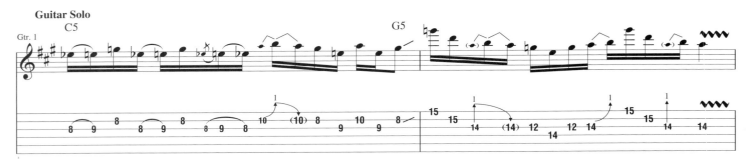

Gtr. 1

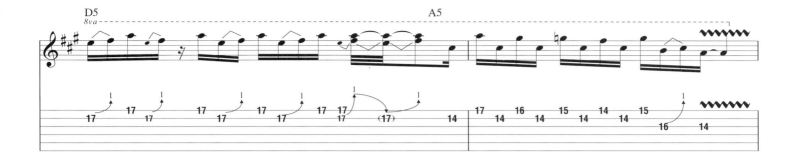

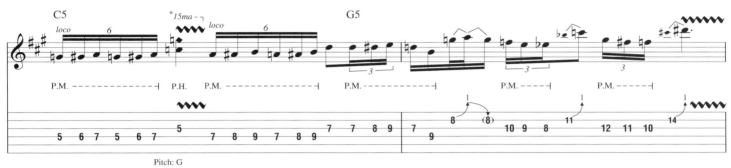

Pitch: G

* Refers to harmonic only

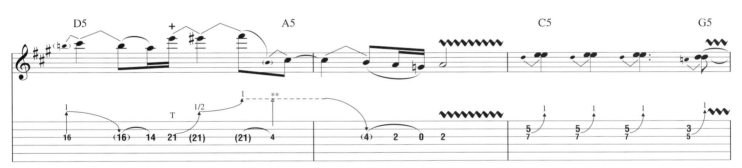

** Move L.H. down to the 4th fret while holding bend with R.H. finger.

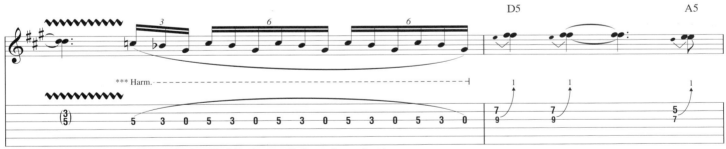

*** Lightly rest the edge of the R.H. palm perpendicular to and across the strings.
Starting at the pickups, steadily slide the palm down the fretboard while the L.H. performs the indicated pulloffs.

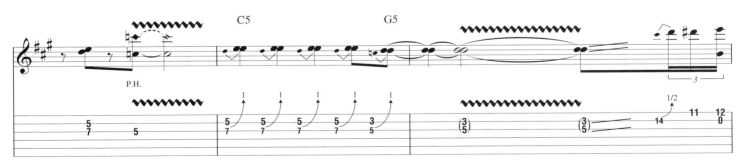

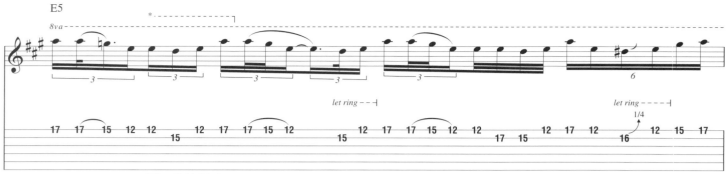

E5

*Played behind the beat.

Bridge

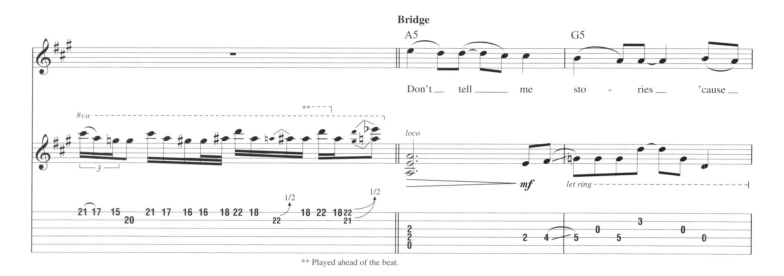

A5   G5

Don't tell _____ me sto - ries _____ 'cause _____

** Played ahead of the beat.

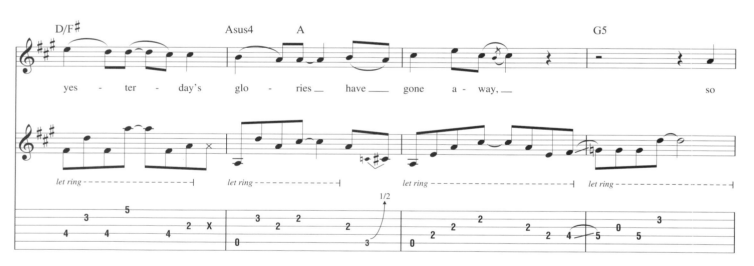

D/F♯   Asus4   A   G5

yes - ter - day's glo - ries _____ have _____ gone a - way, _____ so

Dadd4/F♯   A   G5

far a - way. _____ I've _____ heard _____ it said _____ there's _____ a _____

76

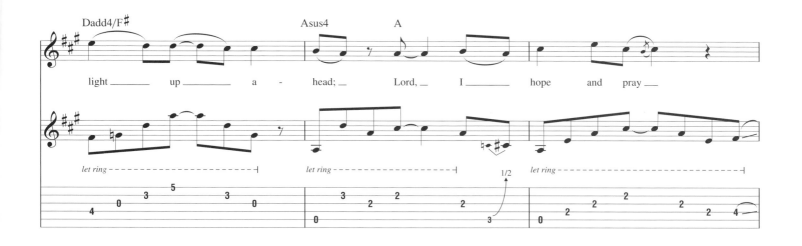

light ____ up ____ a - head; Lord, I ____ hope and pray ____

I'm here to stay, ____ yeah. ____

Interlude

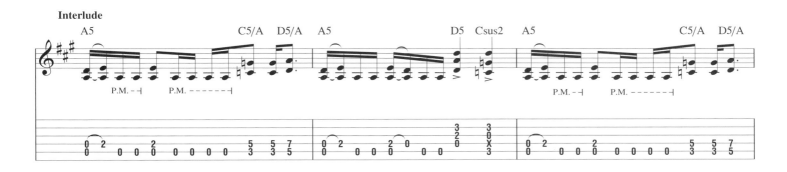

Verse

3. Tell me I'm a sin - ner, I got news ___ for ___ you,   I

Pitch: G A   G

spoke to God this morn - ing and He don't like you. Don't you try ac - cuse me no o -

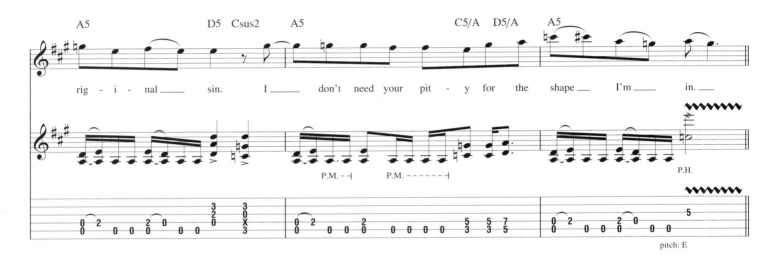

rig - i - nal sin. I don't need your pit - y for the shape I'm in.

pitch: E

Chorus

Gtr. 1: w/ Rhy. Fig. 1 (1 1/2 times)

I don't wan - na change the world, I don't want the world to change

me. I don't wan - na change the world, I

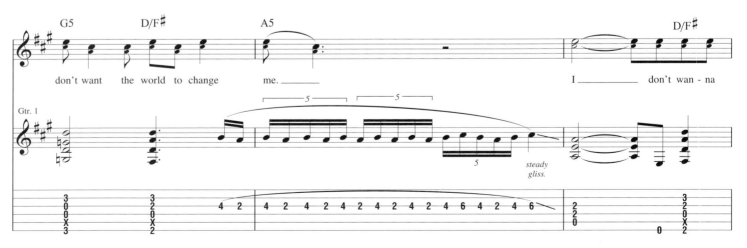

don't want the world to change me. I don't wan - na

Gtr. 1

IN THIS RIVER

Written by
Zachary Wylde

Verse

Gtr. 1: w/ Rhy. Fig. 1 (3 times)
1st time, Gtr. 4 tacet
2nd time, Gtr. 2 tacet
2nd time, Gtr. 3: w/ Fill 1

1st time Gtr. 2 tacet

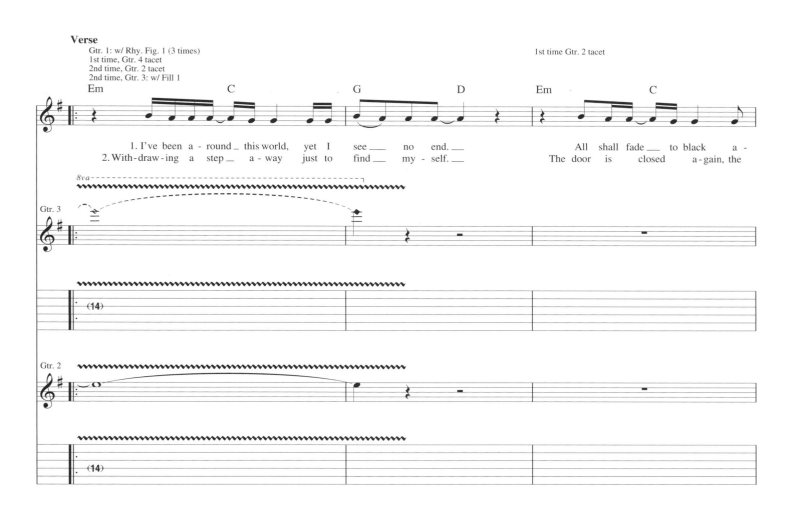

1. I've been a - round this world, yet I see no end. All shall fade to black a -
2. With-draw-ing a step a - way just to find my - self. The door is closed a-gain, the

gain and a - gain.
on - ly one left.

This storm that's bro - ken me, my on - ly friend. Yeah.

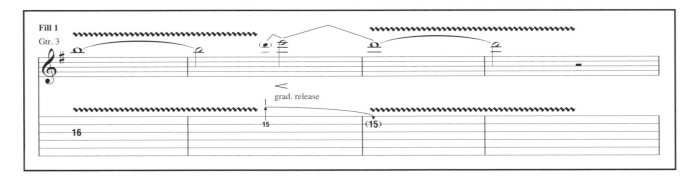

Fill 1
Gtr. 3

grad. release

81

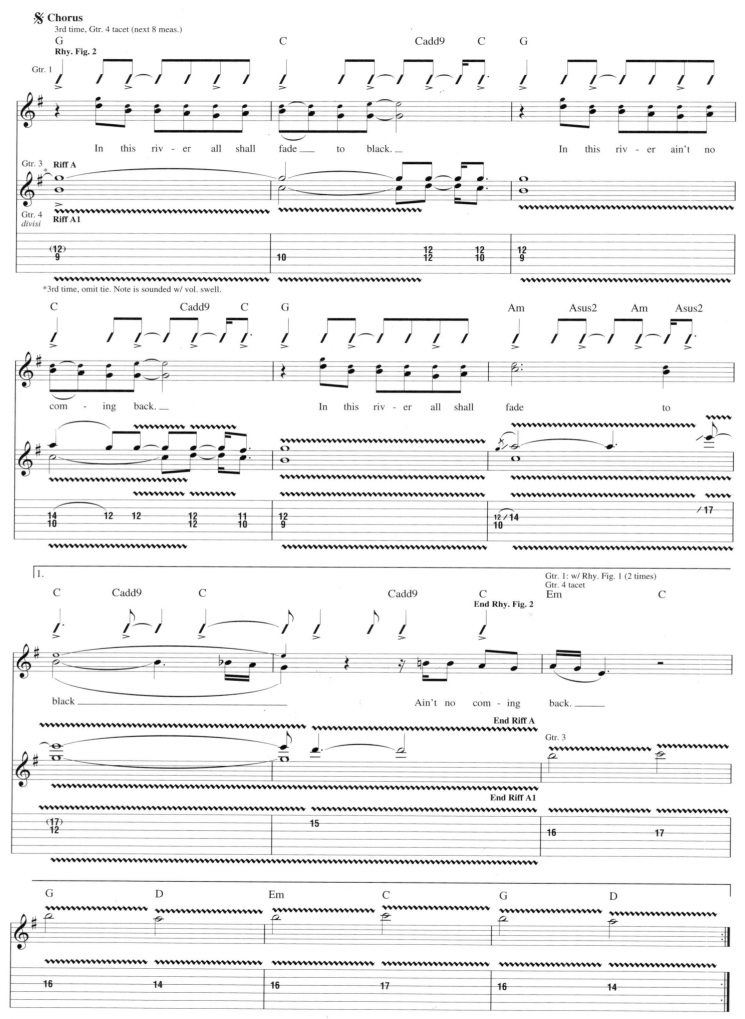

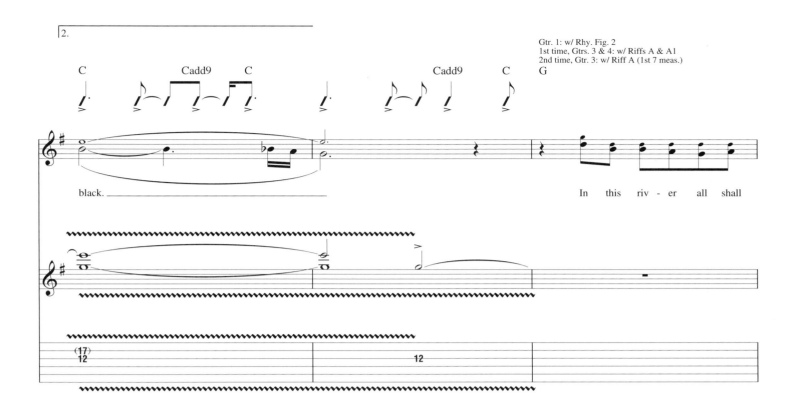

Guitar Solo

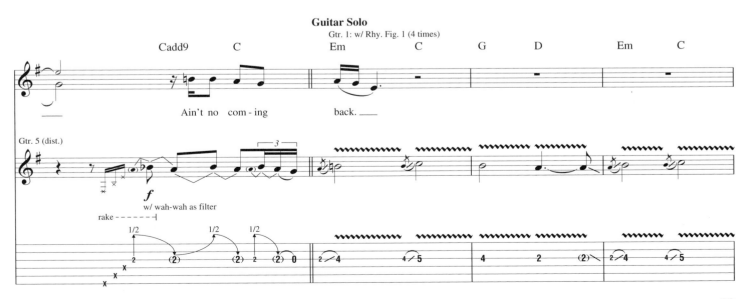

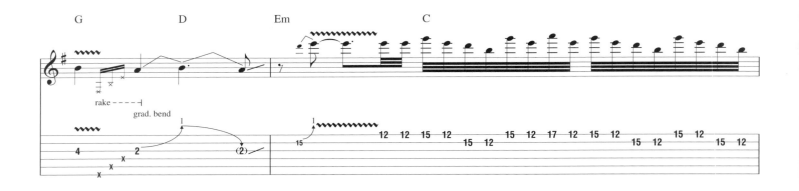

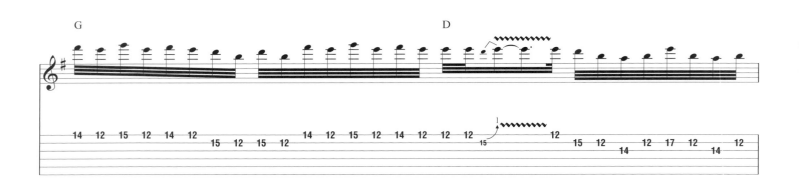

D.S. al Coda
(take 2nd ending)

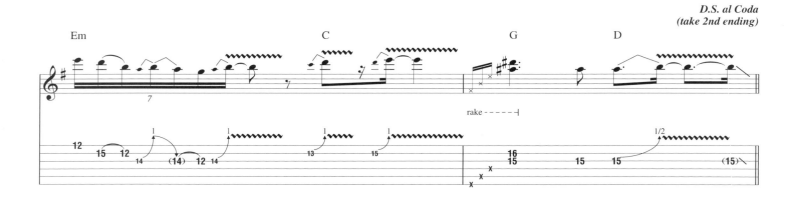

✛ **Coda**

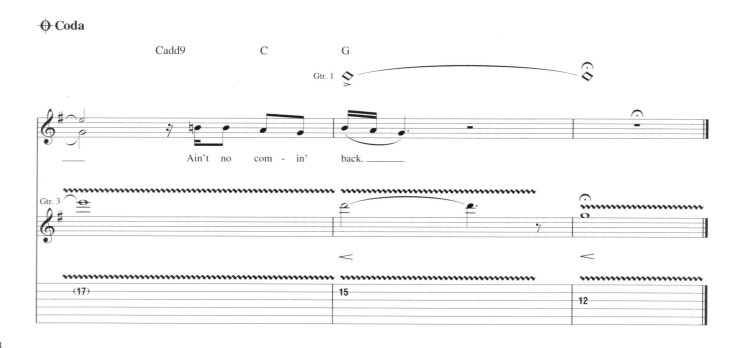

Ain't no com - in' back. _____

LORDS OF DESTRUCTION

Written by Zachary Wylde

Drop B tuning, down 1 step:
(low to high) A-G-C-F-A-D

Intro
Moderately fast ♩ = 148
Half-time feel

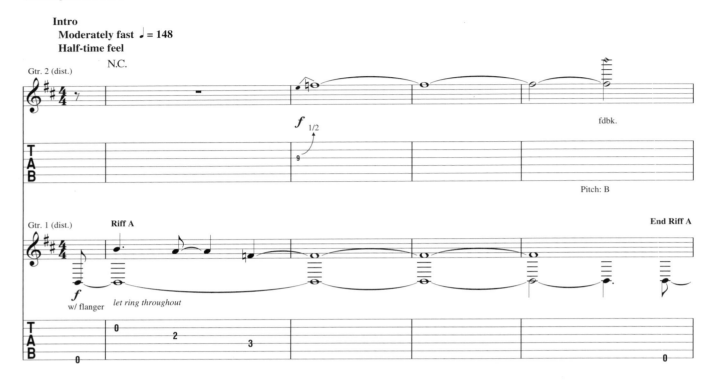

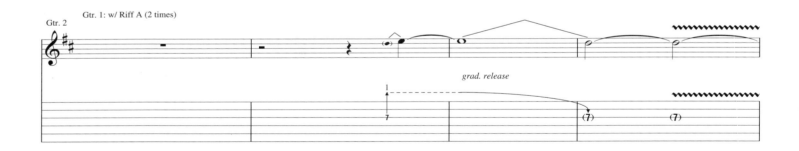

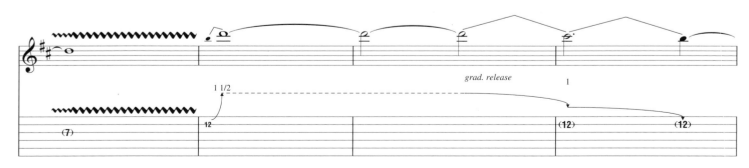

88

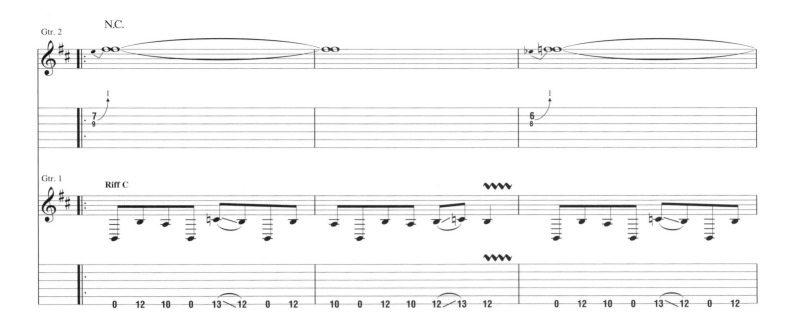

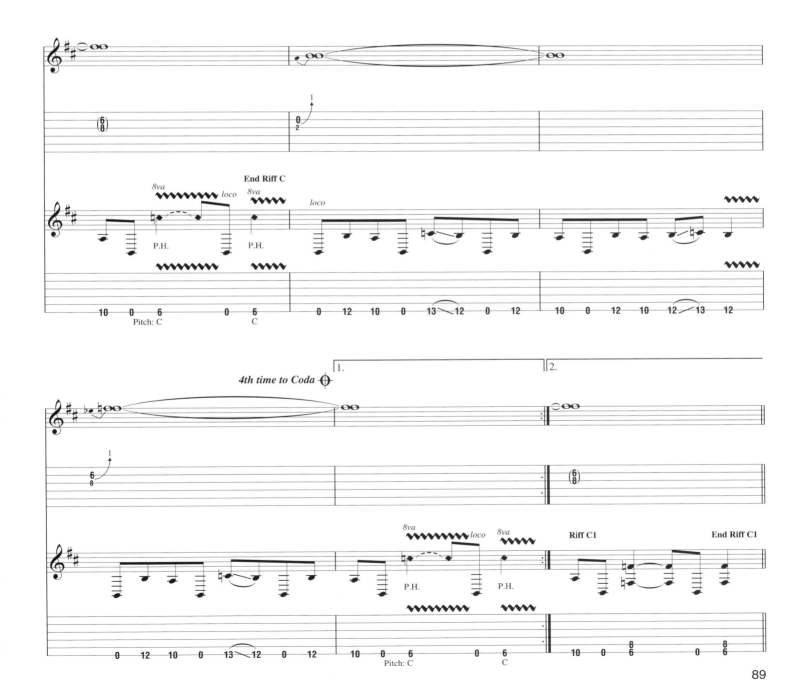

90

Guitar Solo

N.C.

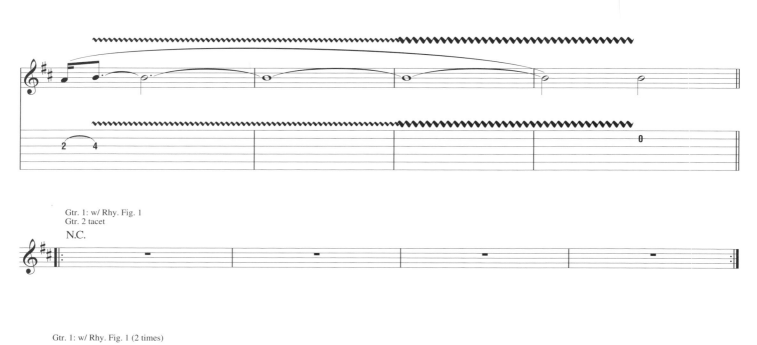

Gtr. 1: w/ Rhy. Fig. 1
Gtr. 2 tacet

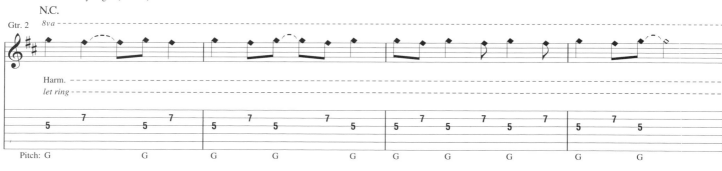

Gtr. 1: w/ Rhy. Fig. 1 (2 times)

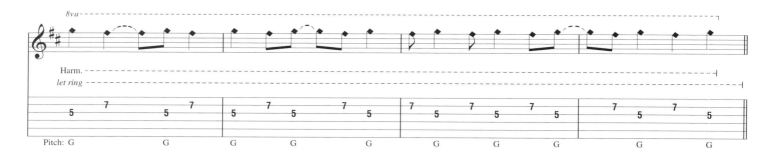

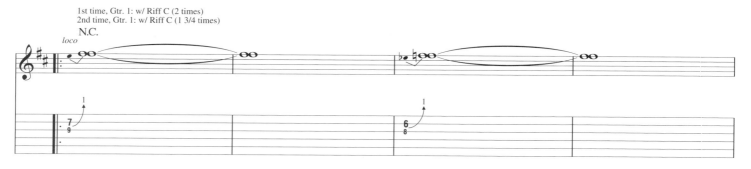

1st time, Gtr. 1: w/ Riff C (2 times)
2nd time, Gtr. 1: w/ Riff C (1 3/4 times)

2nd time, Gtr. 1: w/ Riff C1

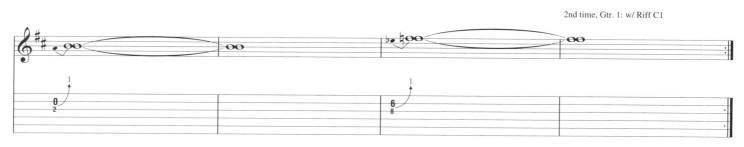

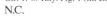

Gtr. 1: w/ Rhy. Fig. 1 (till end)

N.C.

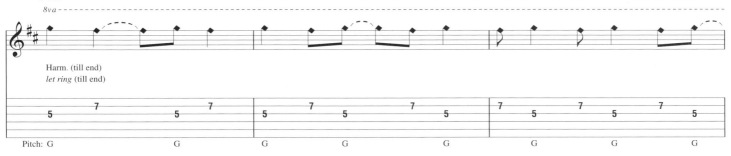

Harm. (till end)
let ring (till end)

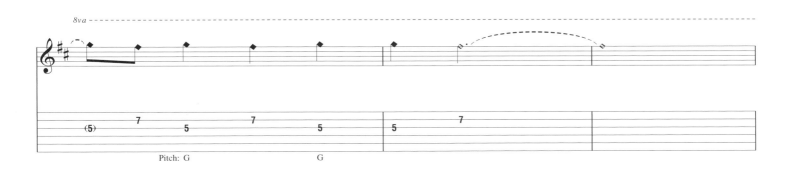

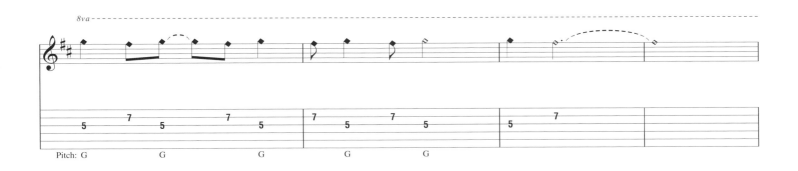

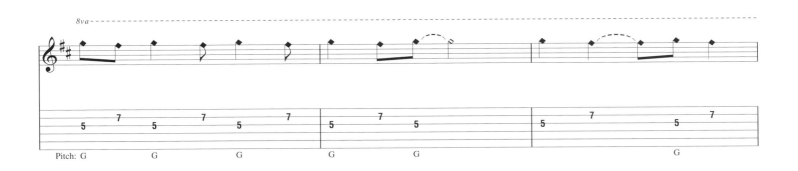

LOSIN' YOUR MIND

Written by Zachary Wylde

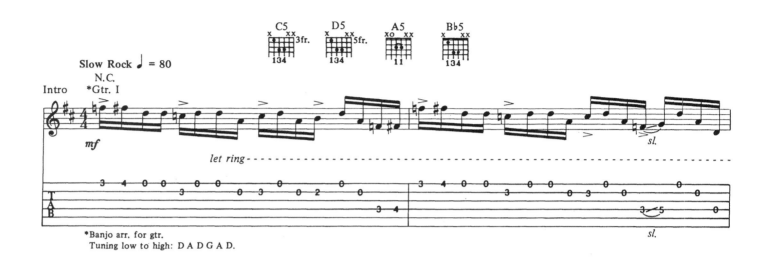

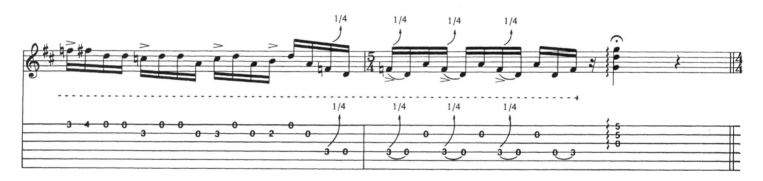

*Tune down: ⑥ = D (All other stgs. tuned normally.)

Lord, I woke up ear-ly this a morn-in'. And as I looked a-round, my

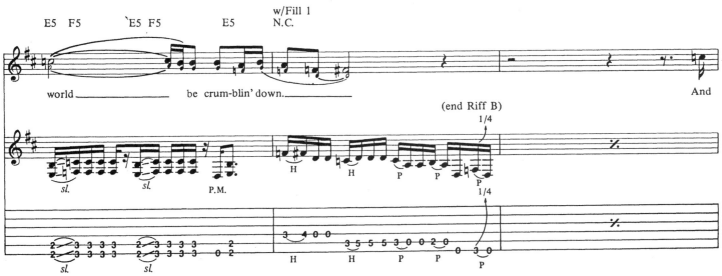

world _____ be crum-blin' down. _____ And

what I saw, well, I could - n't be - lieve.___ Who are you? What might I ___ be?

Things _____ a be - a go-ing on.___ A - go - in' on, ___ ba - by.

Stare at the sun.___ One means three.___ You're at the helm ___ of ___ in -

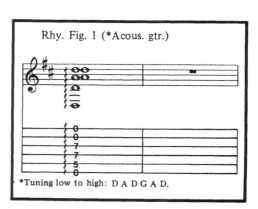

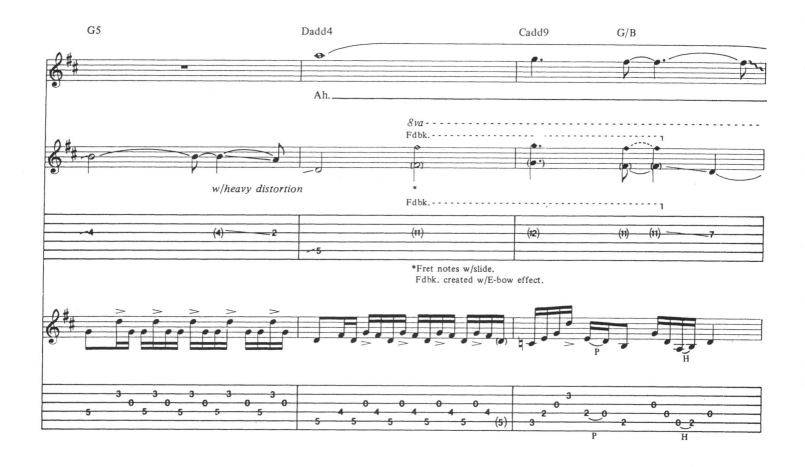

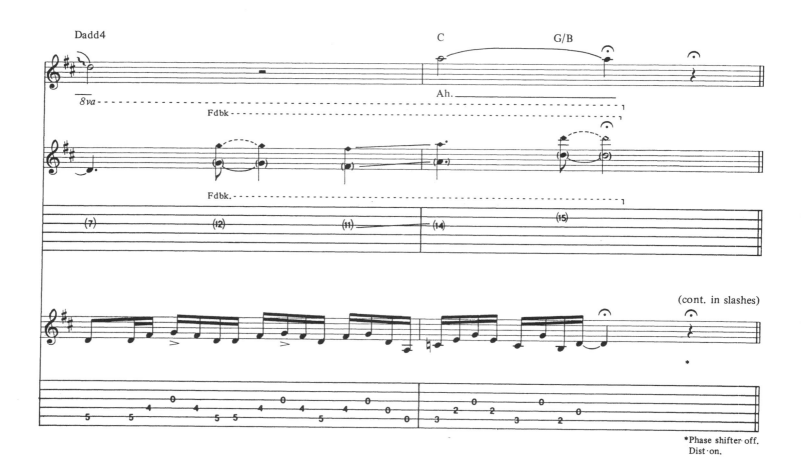

MAMA, I'M COMING HOME

Words and Music by
Ozzy Osbourne and Zakk Wylde

106

107

I've seen your face __ a hun - dred times __
I've seen your face __ a thou - sand times __

ev - 'ry day __ we've been a - part. __

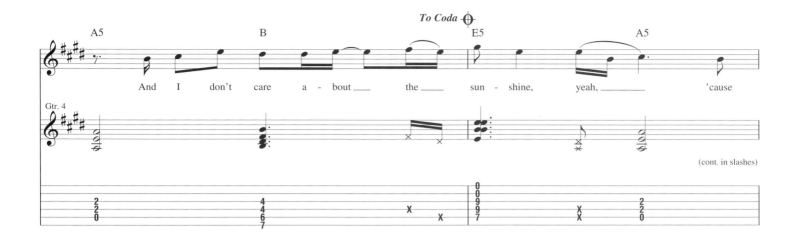

And I don't care a - bout ___ the ___ sun - shine, yeah, _____ 'cause

Gtr. 4

(cont. in slashes)

Chorus

Ma - ma,   Ma - ma, I'm ___ com - ing home. _____

(Home. _____

Gtr. 1

Rhy. Fig. 2

I'm com - ing home. _____

Home.) _____

End Rhy. Fig. 2

Gtrs. 1 & 4

P.M. - |

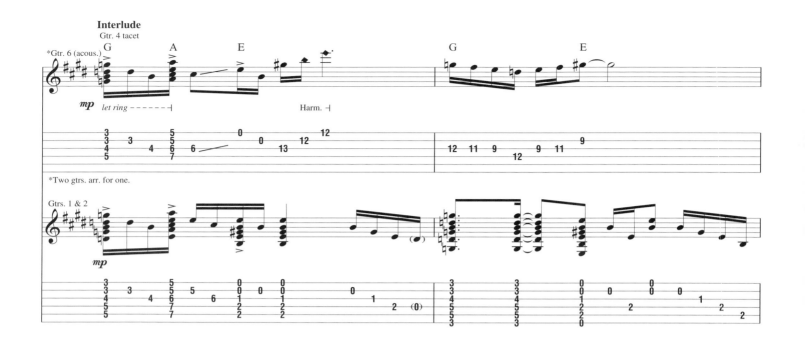

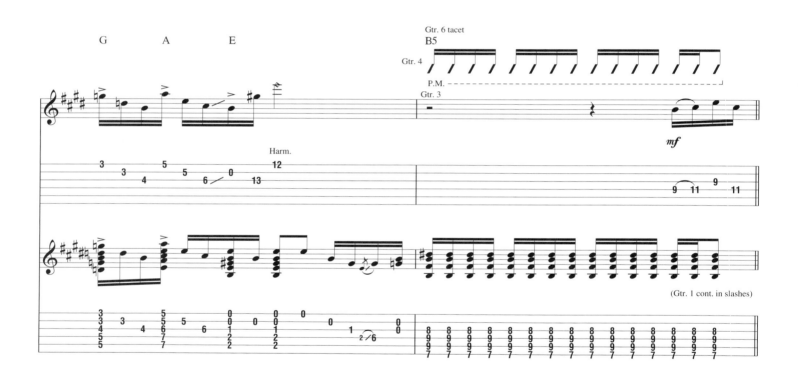

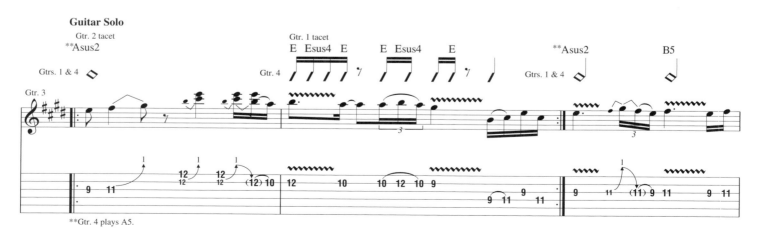

MIRACLE MAN

Words and Music by Ozzy Osbourne,
Zakk Wylde and Bob Daisley

NO MORE TEARS

Words and Music by Ozzy Osbourne,
Zakk Wylde, Randy Castillo,
Michael Inez and John Purdell

1. The light in the win-dow is a crack in the sky. _____
3. ... now that it's o - ver, can we just say good-bye? _____

A stair-way to dark-ness in the blink of an eye. _____
I'd like to move on ___ and make the most of the night. _____

A le - vee of tears ___ to learn she'll
May - be a kiss ___ be - fore I

*Gtr. III tuned the same as Gtr. I.

*Tuned down 1/2 step.

*Recitation: It's just a sign of the times. Going forward in reverse.
Still, he who are first, is just a hand in the bush.

SOLD MY SOUL

Written by Zachary Wylde

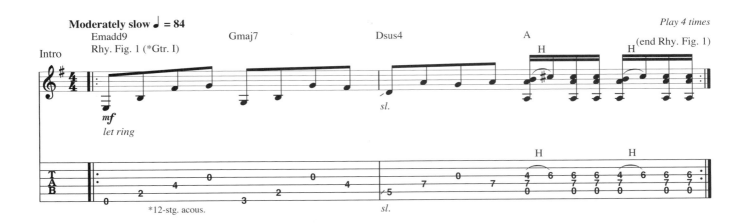

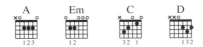

1. con-tem-plat-ing su-i- cide, torn___ from all my___ pride.___ A man tells me, "Son,___ that ain't the___

___ way. I'm gon-na make a deal__ with you__ child. Gon-na live an-oth- er__ day. Just

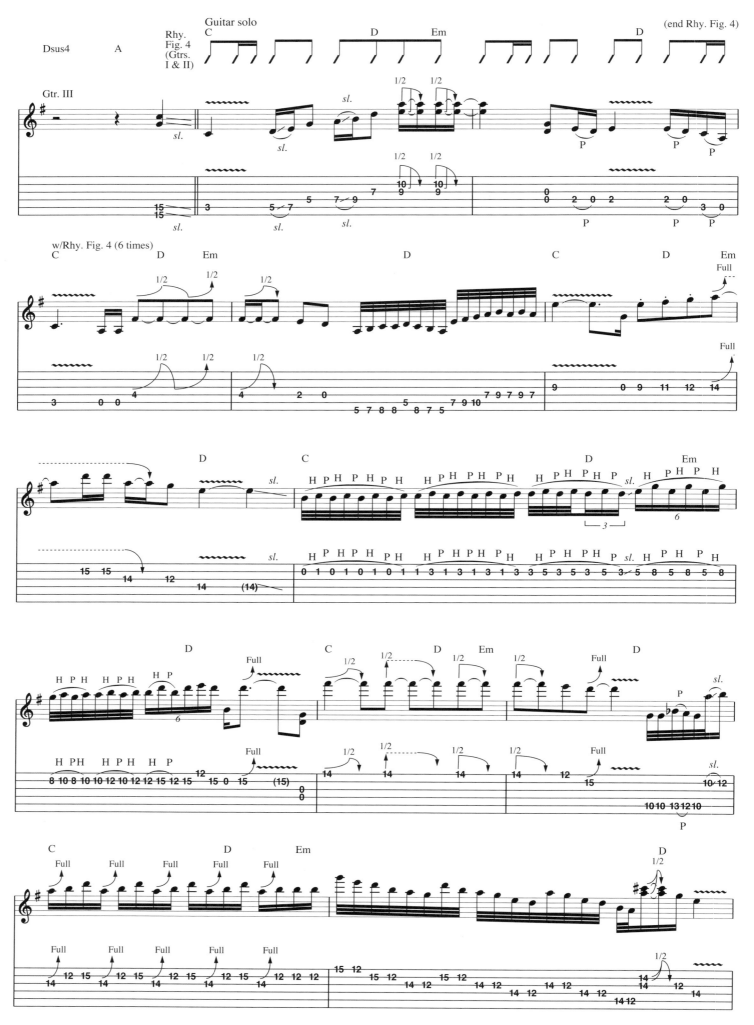

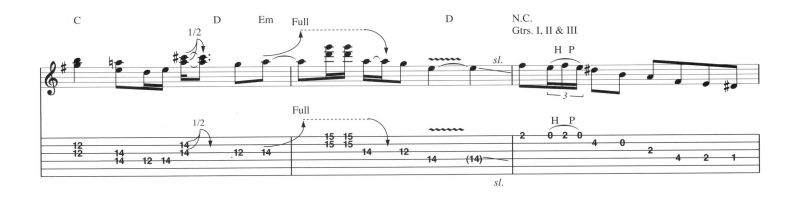

D.S. al Coda

Just sign____ right here____ son.   Ev-'ry-thing will be al -

Outro/Guitar solo
w/Rhy. Fig. 3 (8 times)

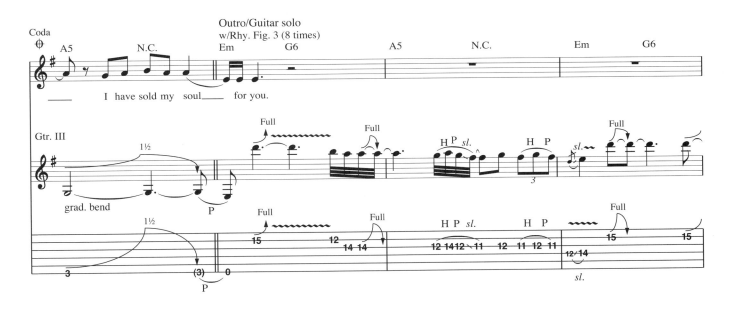

____ I have sold my soul____ for you.

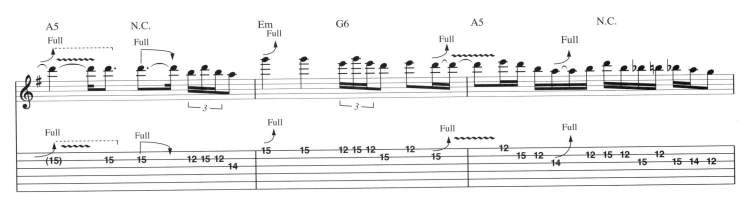

131

Additional Lyrics

2. I was told by this man it would be worth my while.
   He'd return me to my woman, return me to my smile.
   It's all I ask for in this life.
   Whatever's wrong, son, he told me he'd make right.
   Just sign right here, child; everything will be alright. *(To Chorus)*

SPEEDBALL

Written by Zachary Wylde

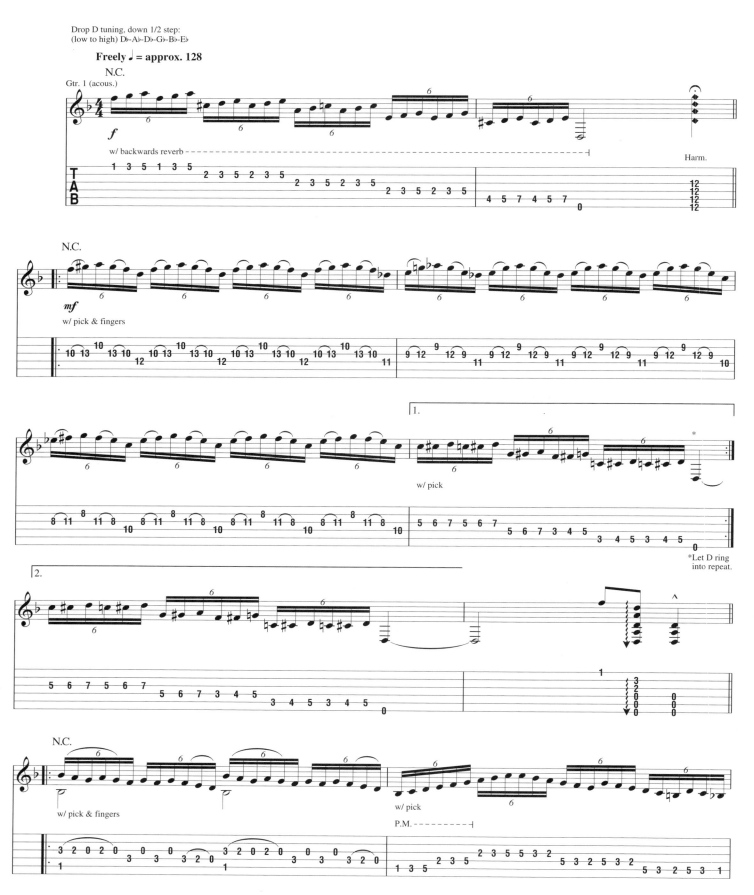

STILLBORN

Written by Zachary Wylde

*Bass plays D.

**Approx. fret position;
slide into neck pickup.

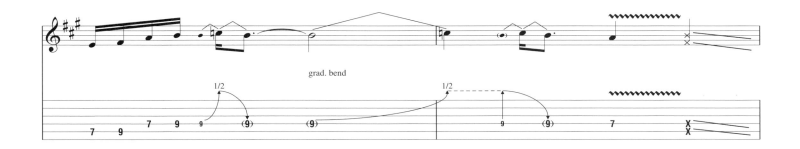

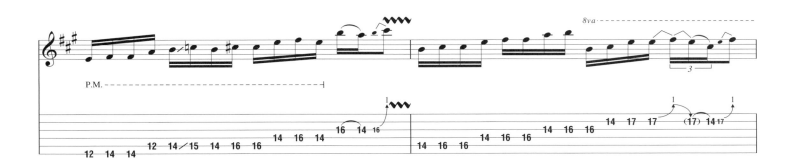

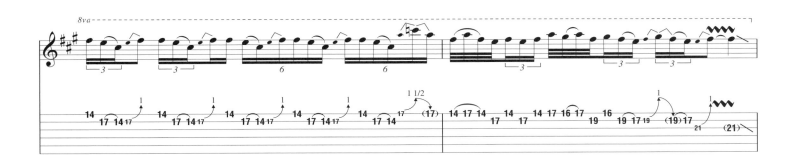

D.S. al Coda
(take 2nd ending)

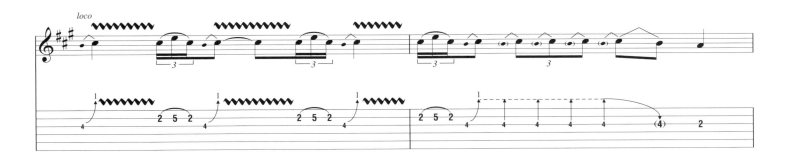

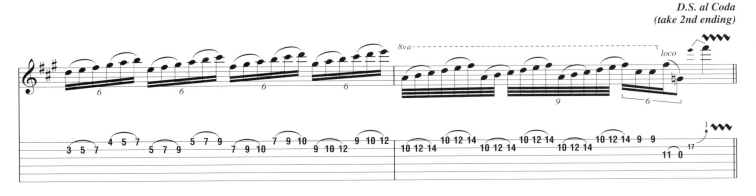

STRONGER THAN DEATH

Written by Zachary Wylde

End half-time feel

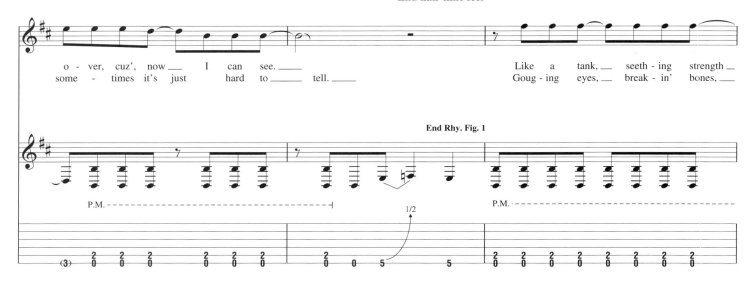

End Rhy. Fig. 1

o - ver, cuz', now ___ I can see. ___ Like a tank, ___ seeth - ing strength ___
some - times it's just hard to ___ tell. ___ Goug - ing eyes, ___ break - in' bones, ___

___ crush - ing all, ___ pull - ing you un - der my treads. ___
___ eat - in' flesh ___ puts a smile ___ on my face. ___

Lost some years, ___ lost some days, ___ that's O. K., ___ I piss on what's ___ in my ___
Crawl - in' through grass, ___ eat - in' nails, ___ los - in' blood, ___ it's all part of find - in' your ___

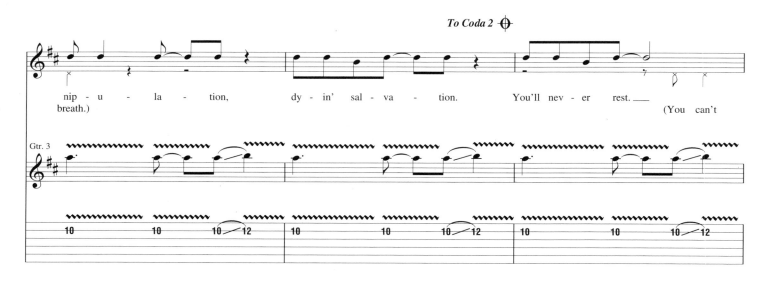

nip - u - la - tion, dy - in' sal - va - tion. You'll nev - er rest. ___

breath.) (You can't

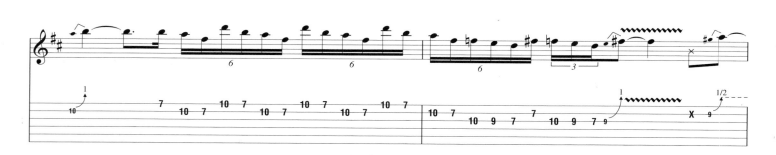

kill what's strong - er than death.)

Gtr. 4 (dist.)

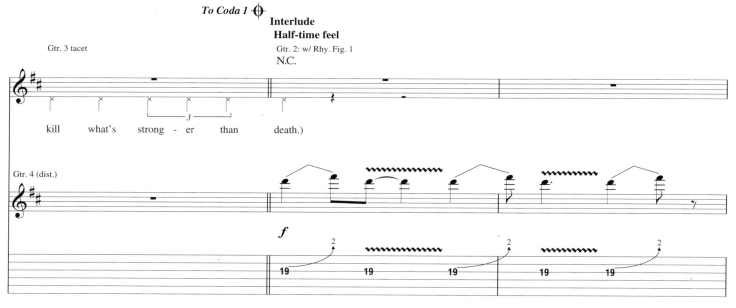

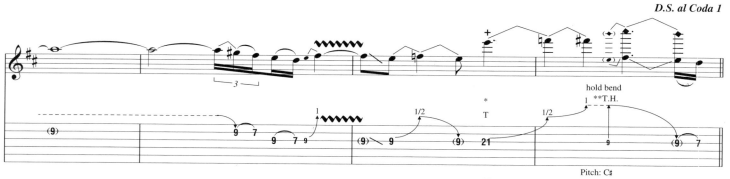

Pitch: C#

*Tap and hold note w/ R.H.   **Tapped harmonic
while bending string w/ L.H.

Coda 1

Guitar Solo
Half-time feel

Gtr. 2: w/ Rhy. Fig. 1

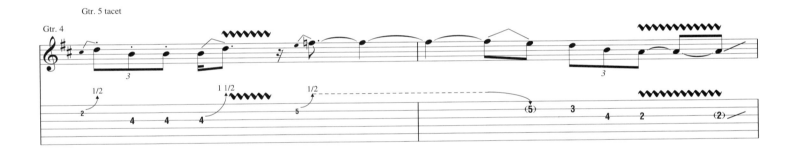

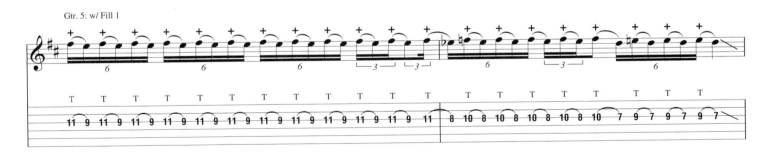

End half-time feel

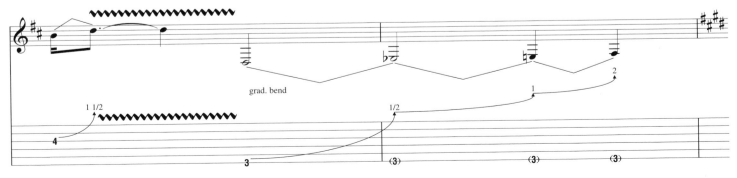

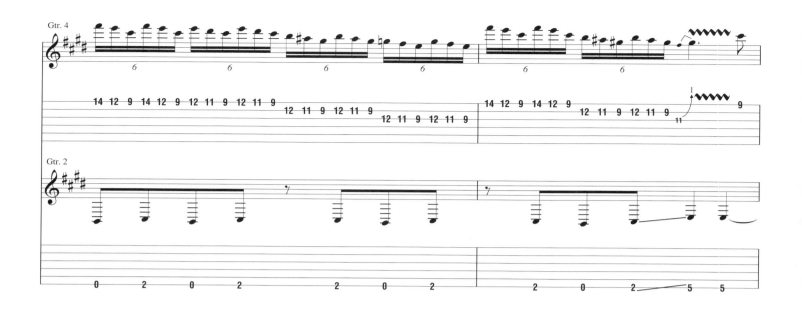

*Tap and hold note w/ R.H. while fretting and
bending note w/ L.H. (next 3 meas.)

148

SUICIDE MESSIAH

Written by
Zachary Wylde

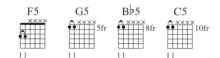

Drop D tuning, down 1 step:
(low to high) C-G-C-F-A-D

Intro
Moderately slow Rock ♩ = 76

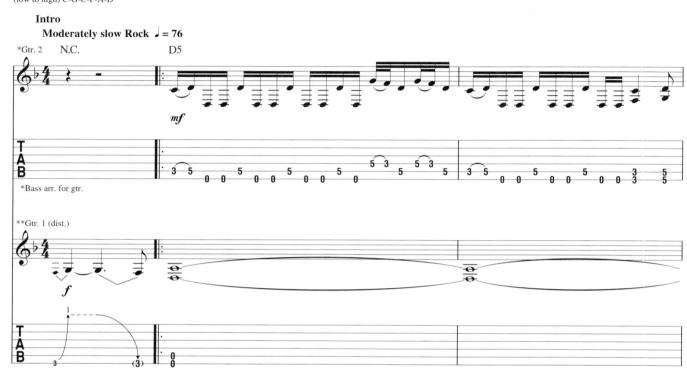

*Bass arr. for gtr.

**Gtr. 1 (dist.)

**Two gtrs. arr. for one.

1. Crawl through the flames that eat___ your flesh._____ Drowned in the wa - ters that know___ you best._____ }
2. Walk through the streets that know___ your name._____ All that's pure is now___ in - sane._____ }

Step in - side, I've been wait - ing here___ for you,___ *(you,___ you.) ___ {An -

*Echo repeats

On your knees where you___ shall crawl._____ Fly - ing so high, you'll nev - er fall._____ }
oth - er trip, an - oth - er lie._____ Life's hand of doom has you feel - ing fine._____ }

Step in - side, we've been wait - ing here___ for you,___ ** (you,___ you.) ___

**Echo repeats.

151

Oh, yeah.

P.M.--

Gtr. 1: w/ Rhy. Fig. 1

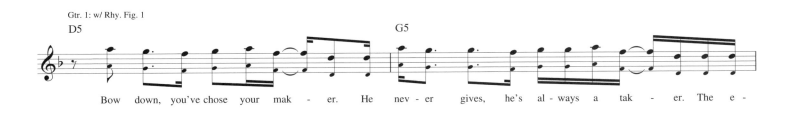

Bow down, you've chose your mak - er. He nev - er gives, he's al - ways a tak - er. The e -

lec - tric burns that fuel the fire. _____ It's just your su - i - cide _____ mes - si -

Gtr. 1

1.

2.

Gtr. 1: w/ Riff A (2 times)
1st time, Gtr. 3: w/ Fill 1

1st time, Gtrs. 4 & 5: w/ Fills 2 & 2A

N.C.

- ah. _____

Gtr. 6 (dist.)

f
don't
pick

X\12/17\15/19 8/17\15/19

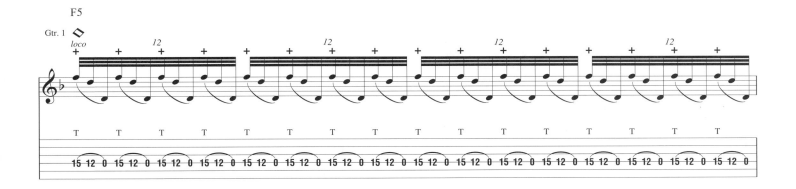

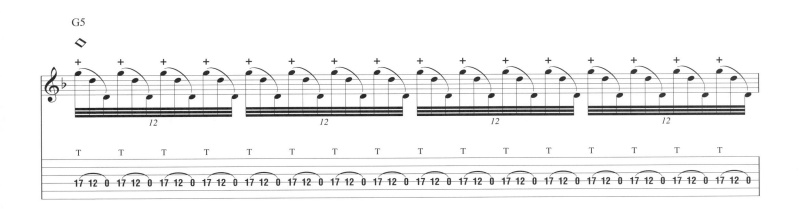

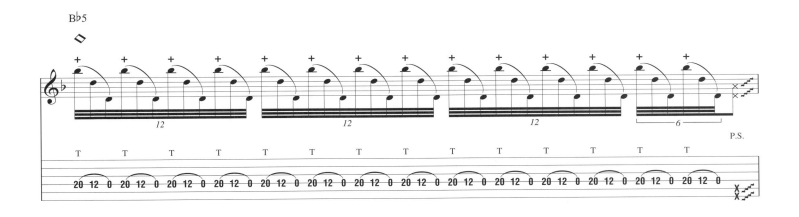

Gtr. 1: w/ Rhy. Fig. 1

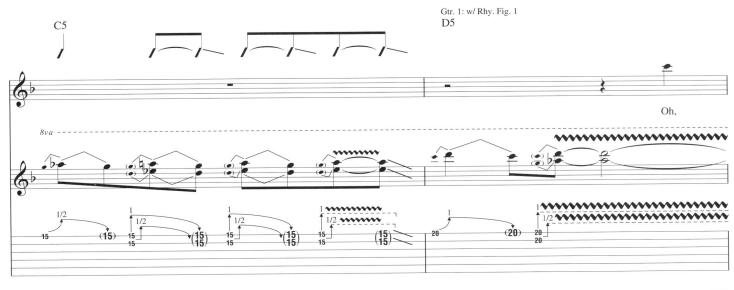

Oh,

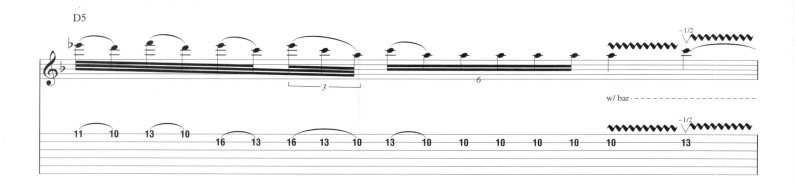

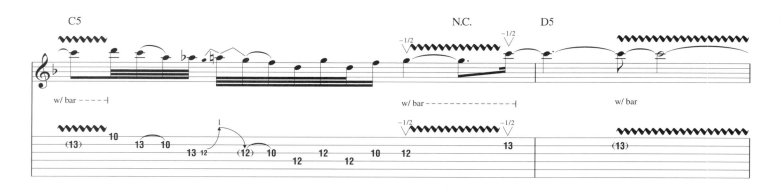

Begin fade

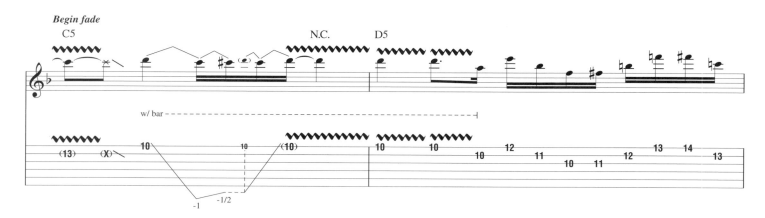

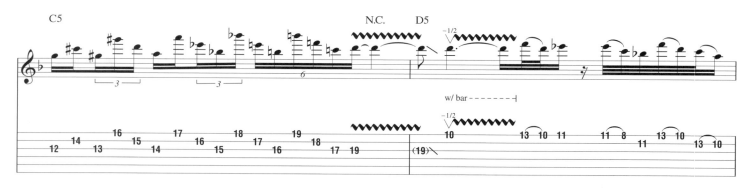

Fade out

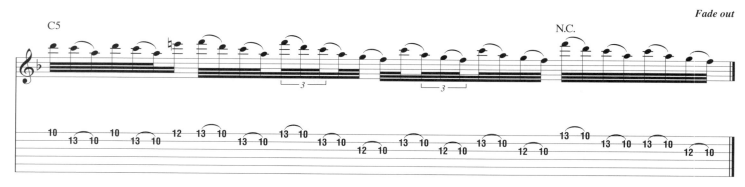

SUPERTERRORIZER

Written by Zachary Wylde

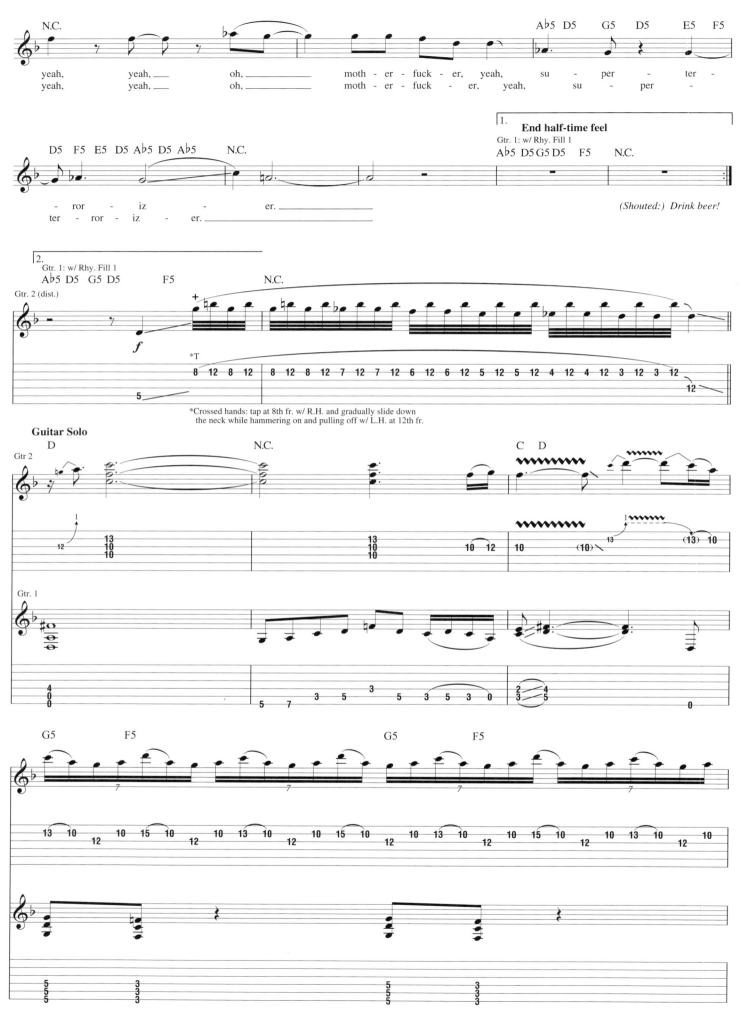

164

*Tap and hold note w/ R.H. while bending note w/ L.H.,
 then hold bend w/ L.H. while pulling off.

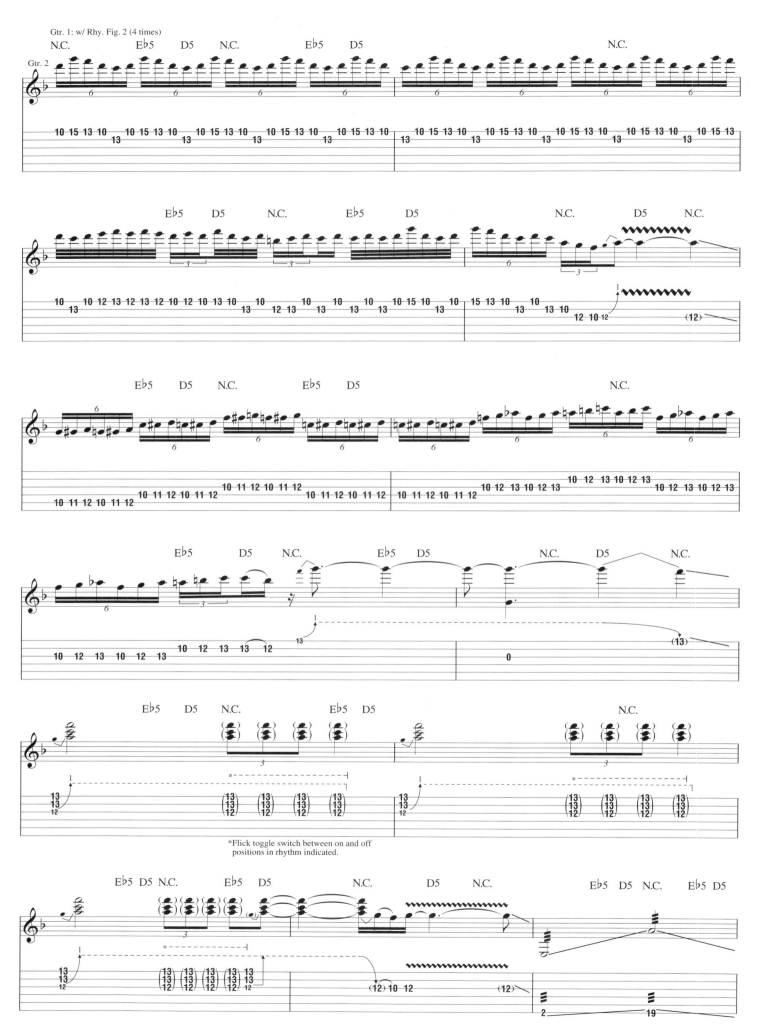

*Flick toggle switch between on and off
positions in rhythm indicated.

GUITAR NOTATION LEGEND

Guitar music can be notated three different ways: on a *musical staff*, in *tablature*, and in *rhythm slashes*.

RHYTHM SLASHES are written above the staff. Strum chords in the rhythm indicated. Use the chord diagrams found at the top of the first page of the transcription for the appropriate chord voicings. Round noteheads indicate single notes.

THE MUSICAL STAFF shows pitches and rhythms and is divided by bar lines into measures. Pitches are named after the first seven letters of the alphabet.

TABLATURE graphically represents the guitar fingerboard. Each horizontal line represents a string, and each number represents a fret.

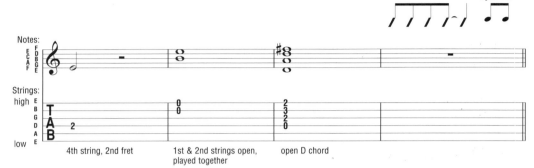

4th string, 2nd fret | 1st & 2nd strings open, played together | open D chord

HALF-STEP BEND: Strike the note and bend up 1/2 step.

WHOLE-STEP BEND: Strike the note and bend up one step.

GRACE NOTE BEND: Strike the note and immediately bend up as indicated.

SLIGHT (MICROTONE) BEND: Strike the note and bend up 1/4 step.

BEND AND RELEASE: Strike the note and bend up as indicated, then release back to the original note. Only the first note is struck.

PRE-BEND: Bend the note as indicated, then strike it.

VIBRATO: The string is vibrated by rapidly bending and releasing the note with the fretting hand.

WIDE VIBRATO: The pitch is varied to a greater degree by vibrating with the fretting hand.

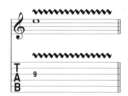

HAMMER-ON: Strike the first (lower) note with one finger, then sound the higher note (on the same string) with another finger by fretting it without picking.

PULL-OFF: Place both fingers on the notes to be sounded. Strike the first note and without picking, pull the finger off to sound the second (lower) note.

LEGATO SLIDE: Strike the first note and then slide the same fret-hand finger up or down to the second note. The second note is not struck.

SHIFT SLIDE: Same as legato slide, except the second note is struck.

TRILL: Very rapidly alternate between the notes indicated by continuously hammering on and pulling off.

TAPPING: Hammer ("tap") the fret indicated with the pick-hand index or middle finger and pull off to the note fretted by the fret hand.

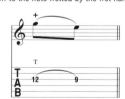

NATURAL HARMONIC: Strike the note while the fret-hand lightly touches the string directly over the fret indicated.

PINCH HARMONIC: The note is fretted normally and a harmonic is produced by adding the edge of the thumb or the tip of the index finger of the pick hand to the normal pick attack.

PICK SCRAPE: The edge of the pick is rubbed down (or up) the string, producing a scratchy sound.

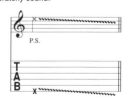

MUFFLED STRINGS: A percussive sound is produced by laying the fret hand across the string(s) without depressing, and striking them with the pick hand.

PALM MUTING: The note is partially muted by the pick hand lightly touching the string(s) just before the bridge.

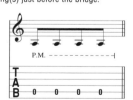

RAKE: Drag the pick across the strings indicated with a single motion.

TREMOLO PICKING: The note is picked as rapidly and continuously as possible.

VIBRATO BAR DIVE AND RETURN: The pitch of the note or chord is dropped a specified number of steps (in rhythm), then returned to the original pitch.

VIBRATO BAR SCOOP: Depress the bar just before striking the note, then quickly release the bar.

VIBRATO BAR DIP: Strike the note and then immediately drop a specified number of steps, then release back to the original pitch.